HOME DESIGN SERIES

Kitchen & Bathroom Ideas

Picture Credits
Allmilmö: 21, 23(l); Armstrong World Industries: 9; Brigitte Baert: 66(l), 96; Bauknecht Domestic Appliance: 57; Ed Baxter: 108/9; Paul Beattie: 31(l), 39, 41(l,r), 56/7, 103(r), 105(r), 106(l); Beckermann Kitchens (UK) Ltd: 35, 42/3; Beekay Kitchen Furniture: 27, 37; Michael Boys: 118(l); Camden Studio: Front cover, 20/1, 28(l), 33(b), 50(b), 70, 72/3, 82, 82/3; Condor Public Relations: 111(l); Crescourt Loft Conversions: 113(r); Dolphin Showers: 76(r); Dorma: 118(r); Ray Duns: 71(r), 83(t), 99(b); Foldor Ltd: 108; Geoffrey Frosh: 38(l); Goldreif Kitchens (UK) Ltd: 40; Greencraft Kitchens: 61, 71(l); C.P. Hart & Sons: 1, 26, 56(b), 64/5, 80, 93(l); Hathaway Country Kitchens: 64; ICI Paints Division: 45; Ideal Standard: 74, 79, 95, 100(b), 115; H&R Johnson Tiles Ltd: 102; The House of Mayfair: 72(b); Dave King: Back cover, 28(r), 30(t&b), 76(l), 86(l), 87, 100(t); Kingfisher Contour: 38; Lancaster Carpets: 93(r), 99(t); Tom Leighton: 67; Max Logan Associates: 2, 66(r); Steve Lyne: 29(b), 97(r), 104, 104/5; Bill McLaughlin: 55(t), 58, 63, 69, 77(r), 114(r), 116, 117(t); Michael Murray: 89; Brian Nash: 7; Neff (UK) Ltd: 19, 25, 48, 49, 60, 65; Nordic: 113(l); Roger Payling: 44, 51(r), 84/5; Poggenpohl (UK) Ltd: 16, 78/9, 88; Spike Powell: 107(r); Prowoda Kitchen Appliances: 8, 52, 53, 54, 59; Malcolm Robertson: 91; Rotaflex Homelighting: 24, 86(r); Sanderson: 73, 111(r); B.C. Sanitan: 103(l), 114(l); SieMatic (UK) Ltd: 15; Smallbone of Devizes: 8/9, 17(r), 18; Jessica Strang: 31(r), 32(tl&b), 33(t), 34, 119; Clive Streeter: 29, 51(l), 117(b); Graham Strong: 94, 106(c); John Suet: 105(l); Steve Tanner: 98; Twyfords Bathrooms: 101; Vogue Bathrooms: 97(l), 110, 112; Gary Warren: 77(l); F. Wrighton & Sons: 4, 6, 11, 12, 13, 17(l), 35, 36, 46/7, 62, 68

Illustrations by Steve Cross, Paul Emra, Kuo Kang Chen, Jim Marks, Venner Artists, Edward Williams Arts.

Author: Maggie Stevenson
Editor: Alison Wormleighton
Designer: Gordon Robertson

Published by Aura Editions
2 Derby Road, Greenford, Middlesex

Produced by
Marshall Cavendish Books Limited
58 Old Compton Street,
London W1V 5PA

ISBN 0 86307 281 X

Typesetting and make-up by
Quadraset Limited, Midsomer Norton,
Bath, Avon

Printed and bound by Grafici Editoriale
Padane SpA, Cremona, Italy

Contents

Introduction

Today we expect more of our kitchens and bathrooms than ever before. As the two most frequently used rooms in the home, their importance is now recognized. The kitchen is the place where, as well as cooking and washing up, people congregate for a chat or to have a cup of coffee, and sometimes also to dine, work or play. As such, it needs to combine practicality with good looks. Bathrooms, too, need to be both efficient and comfortable. They have to be functional enough to allow the whole household to complete their ablutions quickly and conveniently—yet they should also be pleasant, cheerful places where it's nice to spend time simply luxuriating. What is more, both rooms have to be practical and hard-wearing enough to stand up to daily use and keep their looks for years to come.

Not surprisingly, many people's homes haven't caught up with these new developments. Re-fitting a kitchen or bathroom can be a complex and expensive business. Because the fixtures and fittings are long-term investments, they've got to be right first time; you can't afford to make mistakes. In reality, though, careful planning and a little imagination together with a knowledge of the basic ground rules are all you need to create an attractive, workable room.

Of course, you don't have to go all the way and completely re-fit your kitchen or bathroom. There are plenty of inexpensive ways to give either room a face-lift and make it more efficient. Nor do you have to have a huge area to work in. Most people regard their kitchen and bathroom as 'too small'—yet it's when space is at a premium that thoughtful planning and imaginative design will pay the greatest dividends. It is perfectly possible to make a small room efficient and attractive, and even to turn its size to advantage.

So, whether you are seeking the kitchen or bathroom of your dreams, or whether your aims are more modest, this book should help you tailor the rooms to your needs, *and* to your budget. The book is divided into two sections, first kitchens and then bathrooms, and each section begins with that all-important stage of establishing priorities and possibilities (Chapters One and Eight). After that, you'll learn how to turn those ideas into practical reality (Chapters Two and Nine), which is followed by guidelines and tips on making the most of whatever space you have, including fitted kitchens and other methods of storage (Chapters Three and Ten).

Next, the pros and cons of all the different 'surface treatments' are covered, literally from floor to ceiling (Chapters Four and Eleven), followed by details of the latest kitchen appliances and bathroom fittings (Chapters Five and Twelve). After that you'll find ideas for ways to design, decorate and furnish these rooms (Chapters Six and Thirteen), and, finally, there are loads of tips for quick and easy transformations (Chapters Seven and Fourteen). By the end of the book, we hope you will have some concrete ideas and plans for how to improve your kitchen and/or bathroom so it suits you, your family and your lifestyle.

CHAPTER 1

Right from the start

Every cook dreams of the perfect kitchen, where faultless planning, good design and sensitive decoration combine to make a room that is efficient, safe and a pleasure to be in.

The only really well-planned kitchen is the one designed with you, your family and your lifestyle in mind. The tempting pictures in glossy brochures may all look similarly desirable and beautifully organized. But there's no one kitchen that works for everyone. Every cook has her own recipe for perfection.

Establishing priorities

To find it, first you must take a long cool look at your priorities, weigh them against your limitations and temper them with a little realism. The result will be the foundation of a workable kitchen tailored to your needs.

Don't underestimate the importance of this pre-planning stage. Whether you intend to do it yourself or call in the professionals, it is essential to sort out what you really want from your new kitchen. In the long run, forethought saves you money and disappointment.

To work out your priorities, first ask yourself the following questions—when you have evaluated the answers, you'll have a pretty clear idea of the kind of kitchen that will be right for you.

At this stage there's no need to worry about how your kitchen will look. Naturally you'll want it to be interesting and attractive and to reflect your personal style, but the aesthetics can be dealt with after a basic practical plan has been worked out.

Crucial questions

Do you live alone, or as a couple, or do you have a family? Do you spend much time at home?

The number of people in the household directly affects the size and scope of the kitchen required.

A single person can be self-indulgent and design a tightly planned work space where everything is within easy reach.

A couple may decide to be a culinary partnership, in which case they'll have to allow enough room for two people to work as a team going about their tasks without tripping over one another.

A family has an ever-changing variety of needs according to the ages of its members; but however small the family, they will all gravitate to the kitchen, and enough space must be allowed to accommodate them.

Whatever size your household, if your life is largely home-based and you prepare three meals a day and entertain friends at home, you should allow more space for storage and food preparation.

Do you anticipate any major changes in your way of life?

According to recent statistics, most people keep their kitchen for about fifteen years. So if your lifestyle is likely to change in the foreseeable future, plan for those changes at the start.

If you would like to have children, make sure your kitchen will suit them. It must be safe for toddlers, with enough room for them to play nearby without getting under your feet. Warm-to-the-touch flooring, child-proof catches and a large table top for drawing, painting and modelling are all essential when there are small children around. Gadgets that help with cleaning and food preparation are worth the money if they free you to spend time with the family during the growing years.

Going back to work when the children are off your hands? You'll find that with two jobs instead of one, your days have to be planned with military precision. Life will be easier if you keep a good stock of tinned and frozen foods—so allow space to store them. Labour and time-saving equipment like a pressure cooker, microwave oven and dishwasher will suddenly seem more like necessities than luxuries. If you can't afford them right now, leave room so they can be slotted in later.

When retirement is in the offing, the kitchen should be built to last. Have the very best you can afford and make it as convenient as possible, arranging storage so you don't have to bend or stretch too often. Invest in equipment that really will save you effort. Now might be the time to buy a split-level cooker or to swap your chest freezer for an upright one that gives easier access.

What kind of cook are you, creative or convenience? And how many people do you cook for?

The way you cook will be a major influence on your choice of kitchen. If you enjoy experimenting with new ideas

Below: Your kitchen requirements depend upon the size of the household, your cooking habits, your lifestyle and whether you need to use the kitchen for other purposes such as eating meals or studying.

Above: The sort of kitchen equipment you'll need will to a large extent be dictated by your cooking habits. If you do a lot of frying, for instance, a built-in deep fat fryer like this one could be very handy.

and entertain friends to dinner regularly, you'll need clear runs of work surface for food preparation, plus plenty of cupboards. You're bound to have collected a considerable batterie de cuisine as well as special dishes for serving everything from a soufflé to a salmon, and the chances are you'll also have a certain amount of electrical gadgetry. All of it will need convenient, well-organized storage.

Food storage will need careful thought, too. If you like to cook ahead, a good-sized freezer is invaluable. And if you love trying out exotic recipes, you'll have to think up some intelligent way of keeping all the jars of spices and herbs so they're easy to find. When it comes to major equipment the entertaining cook might find a double oven and a dishwasher are worthwhile buys.

If, on the other hand, you regard cooking as a chore and make the most of convenience foods, preferring to go out to a restaurant when there's something to celebrate, a much simpler kitchen will suit you admirably. Under-used expensive equipment will stand as a constant reproach, so, if you don't need it, don't have it.

Some gadgets, however, will be useful even to the unenthusiastic cook. Depending on the kind of food you prefer, a contact grill, a deep fat fryer and a microwave oven might be handy.

What kind of food do you enjoy? Where do you buy it and how often do you shop?

The type of food you like and the way you buy it will also be among the main factors deciding the kind and amount of storage you must allow. Both the convenience cook and the cook who lives a long way from the shops, making infrequent but mammoth expeditions to stock up, need plenty of cupboard space for tinned, dried and packaged food. The gardening cook and anyone with a good regular source of cheap fresh fruit, vegetables, meat or fish will need a freezer big enough to cope with the gluts, and could probably cope with less space for dry stores.

If you like fresh food and you bottle or preserve rather than freeze it, an old-fashioned larder with cool slate or marble shelves would be an asset. Larders are perfect for keeping dairy produce like cheese and eggs so they stay fresh but don't get too cold and vegetables so they stay crisp and don't become 'sleepy'.

The cook whose shopping pattern is fairly regular, buying store cupboard standbys weekly or monthly and fresh food on a day-to-day basis, will have to work out her own storage ratio for perishable and packaged foods.

Do you eat any or all of your meals in the kitchen?

A kitchen which has to double as a breakfast room, family dining room or, indeed, the only dining room, must be designed with that fact in mind from the

Left: If you are accustomed to bulk buying you will need to ensure you have sufficient storage space in your kitchen. Above: A narrow breakfast bar with stools that slide under it is a good way of fitting an eating area into a small space.

Right and below: A handy flap-down breakfast table is not difficult to build. It takes up very little room when folded, and the frame includes some shelves for storage. Facing page: A pull-out table, which slides into the units to keep it clean and out of the way, is useful if you want to use the kitchen for other purposes, such as sewing.

outset. Eating meals in cramped, uncomfortable surroundings is no pleasure.

If the only meal likely to be taken in the kitchen is breakfast and perhaps the occasional snack, a breakfast bar is all you'll need in the way of a table, with stools that can be tucked away under it to provide the seating. Accommodating a bar shouldn't pose a serious planning problem as it won't take up much space. In fact, it could be a positive advantage providing as it does an extra work surface where you can sit down to such jobs as preparing vegetables or polishing silver.

Dining on a larger scale demands a real increase in floor space. If the kitchen as it stands is not big enough for a table and chairs to fit comfortably, it may be worth looking at the possibility of enlarging it. Adjacent areas such as an outdoor wc, a walk-in larder, an old scullery or a coal house could be sacrificed to give the extra space; but if there is no scope for enlarging within the existing house structure, then an extension may be the only practical alternative.

For safety and convenience, the dining area should be quite separate from the work space. While the family won't mind watching food being prepared, when you have guests it is better to screen off the cooking area in some way—nothing spoils the appetite more than the sight of dirty dishes piled up around the sink. Cooking smells, too, can be distinctly off-putting. Eliminate them by making sure the kitchen is properly, and controllably, ventilated.

How many roles must your kitchen play? Is is just a place to cook food or do you expect more of it than that?

Apart from being a part-time dining room, the kitchen may have to perform a number of other roles. It can be a laundry, a study, an office, a sewing room or even a greenhouse. Unless you have a huge kitchen that is used as the family's informal living area, try to move at least some of these activities to other rooms, leaving more space for cooking.

If you're lucky enough to have a utility room, the washing machine, dryer and freezer could all be accommodated in it. Failing that, if there's space to spare in the garage and if the necessary electricity, water supply and drainage are available, put the machines there. In some houses, paradoxically, the kitchen is smaller than the bathroom. If that is the case, laundry equipment could be installed in the bathroom, providing, of course, the electrical safely rules are observed.

As long as there's a writing surface and comparative peace, the kitchen may be the best place for children to do their homework. It's likely to be warmer than their bedroom—and, under the watchful parental eye, without the distraction of toys, work will be finished more quickly, too!

The kitchen might also be the obvious location for a home 'office'. Running even the most modest household involves an alarming amount of paperwork, but if it is properly organized, you can keep it under control. Make room, if you can, for a tiny desk area where you can write letters, pay bills and so on. If that is out of the question, at least spare a couple of shelves for a clearly labelled filing system.

Sewing and dealing with houseplants are both messy jobs—though in different ways—but as it is much easier to clean up afterwards if there's a smooth floor and wipe-clean surfaces, the kitchen is the ideal place for them. However, if either task can be re-located—say to a spare bedroom, utility room or conservatory—then do it, because while these extra activities get in the way of the more usual kitchen chores, they too have to be interrupted when it's time to prepare a meal.

Above: Kitchens can be adapted for a variety of other functions, such as a place to keep plants (they will appreciate the warmth and humidity) or a home office complete with swivel chairs and work table.

How long do you expect to live in your house? Is it a short-term let, your first home or a permanent family base?

This is the last and probably most important question you must ask yourself before designing a new kitchen or changing the old one.

If you live in rented property, even if you have a long tenancy, you probably won't want to spend a great deal on major improvements. Your money would be better spent on equipment that makes life easier now and can be taken with you when you go. Having said that, there are ways you can make better use of an existing kitchen without spending a fortune, and we'll take a look at them in the following chapters.

Home owners who don't regard their house as permanent may still think it wise to invest in a new kitchen. Not only will they have a few years' use out of it but when the time comes to sell, as any estate agent will verify, an attractive kitchen is a great asset.

Although designing a kitchen in the knowledge you'll be moving in a few years is comparatively easy—you can plan it without giving too much thought to future needs—try not to be over self-indulgent. Quirky cooking arrangements may suit you, but the person buying your house might just see them as odd! Play safe with a more conservative approach.

If your house will be your home for the foreseeable future, do things properly. Plan your kitchen carefully, making structural changes if necessary, and equip it with the best you can afford. It is worth dipping into your savings or extending your mortgage to have the things you want. Shortcuts will become a constant and increasing irritation and, for a room you will work in daily for a decade at least, that is false economy.

CHAPTER 2

A matter of planning

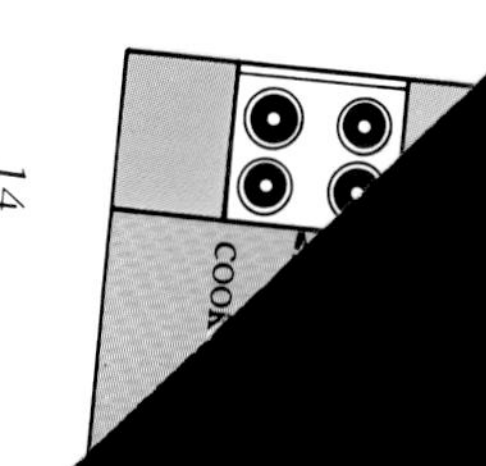

Whether your kitchen is the subject of a major renovation programme or a less ambitious improvement plan, the way it is laid out will be central to its success or failure.

Below: Whatever the shape of your kitchen, you should try to arrange the sink, cooker and fridge in a convenient work triangle, no more than 7m around.

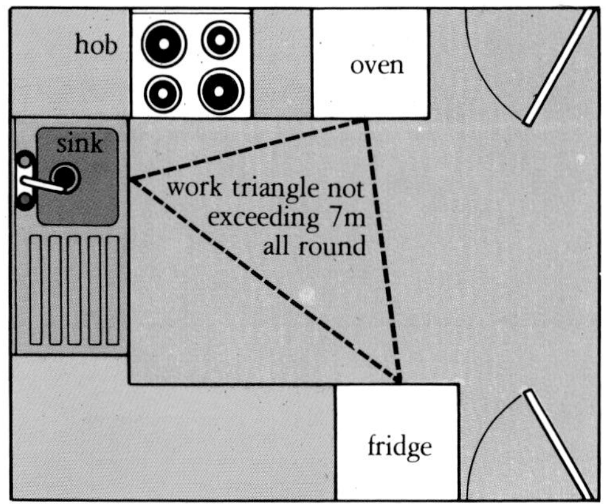

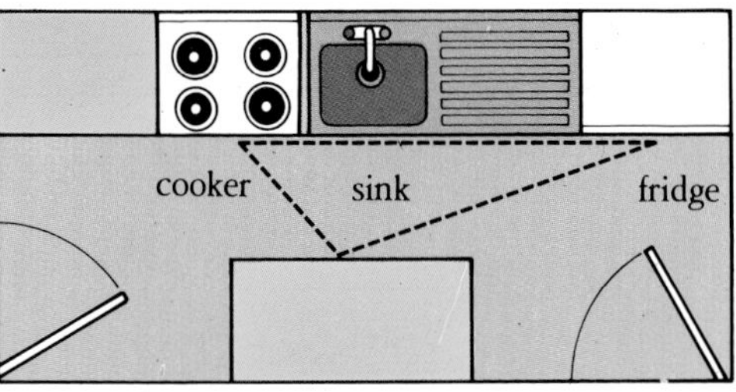

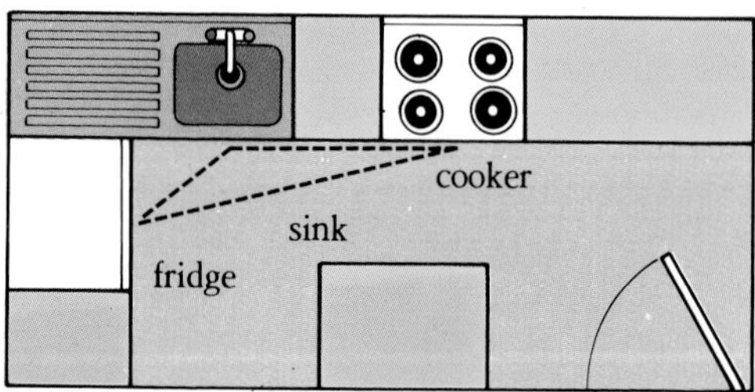

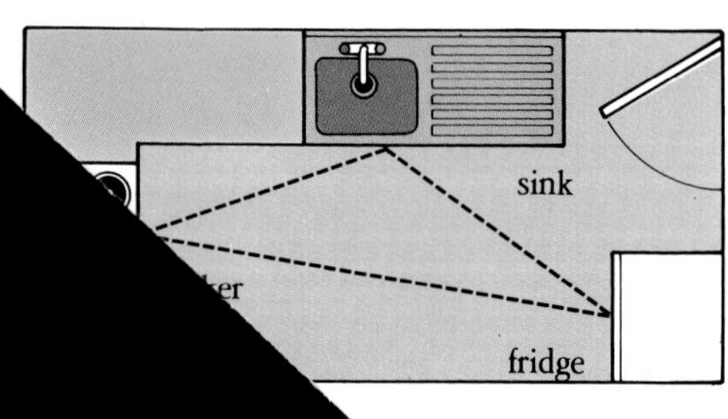

Unlike most other rooms, in the kitchen, the furniture and fittings, once installed, are more or less permanent; and if you don't like the arrangement, you have to either put up with it or involve yourself in even more expense having it changed. Getting it right first time, therefore, is of utmost importance and will be well worth the thought, effort and agony you put into it. (At any rate, planning is half the fun!)

Obtaining advice

If you are buying a complete fitted kitchen from a specialist shop or installer, they will probably design the layout for you. Their consultants are very experienced and will have encountered —and solved—most of the possible problems in the past. Their service is often free, being built into the total cost of the job.

Even so, it is wise to work out a plan of your own before you talk to the consultant. Not only will it give you a chance to familiarize yourself with the advantages and limitations of your own kitchen, but it will enable you to talk things over in a more informed and constructive way.

If you are fitting the kitchen yourself using self-assembly units, you may find the supplier of the units is ready to offer advice or even a fully-fledged planning service. The advice will probably be of a practical kind, helping you to fit all the equipment you want into the given space in a logical arrangement, rather than offering inspired and ingenious solutions to particular problems.

Those aiming to improve their kitchen by revamping existing fittings, and maybe adding to them with some new equipment and extra units, are on their own as far as planning goes. But as it is very much a matter of common sense, even beginners can create a perfectly workable kitchen and one with a great deal of individuality, if they have an understanding of the basic ground rules.

Making plans

Think of it primarily as a functional work space devoted to the preparation and cooking of food and you will have taken an important first step towards building a well-planned kitchen. Like any work space, it must be designed to make the best use of the available commodities which, in this case, are space and the cook's time and energy.

Work triangle

The most successful kitchen layouts are based on the tried and tested 'work triangle'—a concept devised by time-and-motion experts to provide a logical work sequence giving the cook the minimum of leg-work. The three points of the triangle are the main activity zones of food storage, preparation and cooking, and they are linked by runs of work surface.

The food storage area contains the fridge, larder and cupboards for dry stores and tinned goods. The preparation area centres on the sink, and the cooking area on the hob and oven. The space between the storage area and sink is for food preparation; the space between the sink and cooker for mixing foods prior to cooking; and the space at the other side of the cooker for serving.

Ideally, the span between activity zones should be at least 90cm, the route between the three points should be continuous and the total distance round the triangle no more than 7m.

In many kitchens it is impossible to have an unbroken work sequence and, as the two zones most often used in tandem are the preparation and cooking areas, it is better to keep those two areas together and separate the storage area.

To make the triangle work really well, plan your storage sensibly so the things you need are close to hand at the appropriate stage in the cooking process. The following list is intended as a guide to indicate how activity-related storage can improve the work flow. Adapt it to suit the equipment you use and your own method of cooking.

Between the food storage area and the sink, keep everything you need for preparing vegetables such as knives, potato peelers, apple corers, scissors, a chopping board, colander, salad spinner and rubbish bin. Close to the sink you'll also need washing-up equipment; a plastic bowl, dish drainer, washing-up liquid, pan scrubs, washing-up brushes, vegetable brushes, dish cloth and tea towels must all be accommodated. If you can allocate some cupboard space so they can be put away out of sight between times, your kitchen will look much better for it.

The food-mixing area between the sink and cooker is probably the busiest section of the triangle. Here you'll need to keep scales, bowls and basins, measuring jugs, knives, spoons, a food processor, liquidizer, mixer, baking equipment, dry ingredients in regular use such as flour, sugar, rice and so on and oven-proof dishes of various kinds.

Close to the cooker you'll need saucepans, frying pans, wooden spoons, a fish slice and spatula, kitchen paper, foil, seasonings, herbs and spices, oven gloves and special cooking equipment such as a wok, steamer or griddle iron.

At the far side of the cooker is the serving area, where serving dishes, tableware, cutlery, linen, cruet, condiments and trays should be kept.

Incorporating appliances

Once you have decided how storage space will be distributed around the triangle, work out how the major appliances can be incorporated into the

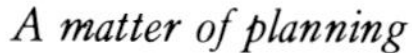

Left: In a well-designed kitchen the area between the hob and sink, which is used for mixing food prior to cooking, should provide an adequate work surface and storage space.

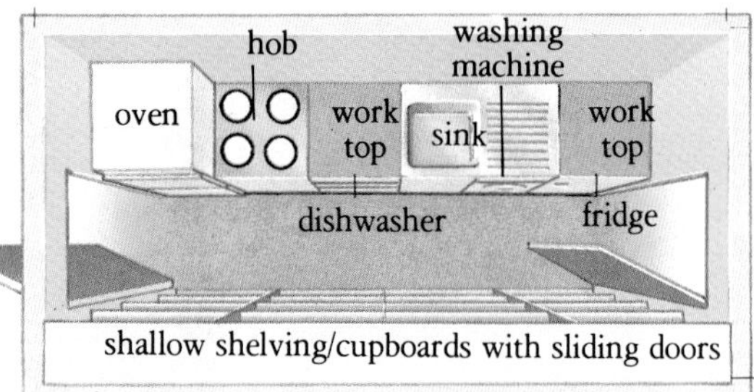

Above: This floor plan shows a narrow galley-shaped kitchen which holds the full complement of appliances. Right: Even in a relatively short straight-line layout, it's possible to fit in a fridge (inside the tall housing unit), dishwasher, sink, hob and oven and still have room for storage.

scheme. Most appliances today are made with fitted kitchens in mind, and the kitchen units are generally based on a standard 600 × 600mm module. (There are also 900mm wide hobs and corresponding cooker hoods and units.) Apart from the cooker, fridge and sink, the other large pieces of equipment you might have to fit in are a freezer, dishwasher, washing machine and tumble dryer.

Their positions will be governed as much by their own operational requirements as their place in the work sequence. Thus, while the freezer fits naturally into the food storage area, access to the water supply and drainage dictates where you can put the washing machine and dishwasher, and the tumble dryer may need to be vented through an outside wall.

A central heating boiler is also very often sited in the kitchen, so this too has to be taken into account. Some are designed to go under worktops like many appliances, while others are worktop height to blend into a run of units as unobtrusively as possible. There are also wall-mounted boilers which leave valuable floor space free for other appliances.

Choosing a layout

Applying the work triangle to a given space may at first seem impossible, but there are a number of standard layouts for units and equipment that will help make the best use of your kitchen whatever its shape.

The straight-line kitchen

This uses the work triangle concept in its purest form, placing the worktop-sink-worktop-cooker-worktop sequence in a single unbroken line. It is the perfect layout for a small room where there is at least one clear wall along which the units and equipment can be ranged. It is useful,

too, in a larger room where cooking is only one of the functions—in a studio apartment or an open-plan family living area, for example.

For safety and ease of working, the straight-line kitchen should be no longer than 7m, and no shorter than 3m. There should be a gangway of at least 1200mm between the front of the units and the opposite wall if two people will be working in the kitchen; a minimum of 900mm should be enough for one cook.

The galley

Similar to the straight-line kitchen but with units running along opposite walls of a long narrow room, this is another arrangement designed to make the most of a small space. Though it makes economic use of the cook's energies by placing everything within easy reach, this layout must be carefully designed to avoid hazards.

Food storage and perhaps a breakfast bar should be on one side of the room with the cooker and sink on the other so there's no danger of spilling liquid or hot food while lifting it between the two. There should be a passage at least 1200mm wide between the units, preferably without doors at either end, as through traffic could cause collisions. Any doors opening into the room should clear the units with 400mm to spare.

The L-shaped kitchen

By ranging the units along two adjacent walls, you can concentrate the work area in quite a tight space, leaving a clear area of floor free for a table and chairs. For safety and convenience, the cooker and sink should share one side of the 'L'.

The only problems with this layout are finding a way of using the rather inaccessible space in the corner of the base units (see pages 34–5 for some possible ways to overcome this problem) and arranging the major appliances so there is still enough space for low-level storage.

The U-shaped kitchen

In a medium-sized, rectangular room, this arrangement works very efficiently. The three activity zones are separated with plenty of work surface between, giving the room a spaciousness conducive to relaxed working. Clever planning, however, will be needed to ensure that the doors of base units on opposite and adjacent sides don't clash with one another, and the problem of using corner space will be doubled (see pages 34–5 for some solutions).

Above left: In an L-shaped kitchen the work zone is along two adjacent walls, leaving the other two walls for the eating area. Above: A U-shaped layout forms a compact and efficient working area.

Peninsular and island kitchens

In a medium to large room, these can make more economic use of space, leaving a greater area free for a dining table. They are both really adaptations of the straight-line or L-shaped layouts described above and can help to make the work triangle more compact.

In the island layout, a separate free-standing block of units is built close to the main line of the kitchen. The island may incorporate food storage and a second sink, making it a self-contained preparation area, or it may house a sink and hob as a tightly planned preparation and cooking zone. An extractor hood or a suspended storage system fitted overhead makes even better use of available space.

The peninsular layout is rather like the U-shaped kitchen but instead of being arranged round three walls, one side of the U projects into the room, making a barrier between the cooking and eating areas. Being double-sided, the peninsula provides scope for more storage; and, if a wide shelf is fixed at a suitable height on the room side, it can also be used as a breakfast bar.

Third dimension

While you're deciding on a floor plan, don't forget that kitchens are three-dimensional and the height of the fittings must be taken into consideration at the same time as the layout.

When you are choosing units, bear in mind that a standard height has been calculated to suit most people. For base units this is generally 900mm (or sometimes 850mm). If you are taller or shorter than average, you can adjust the height for your own comfort by increasing or reducing the depth of the plinth or by choosing wall-hung units, which can be fixed at any level you want.

If you do plan to alter the height of the worktop, keep in mind the fact that the

Facing page: An island layout makes full use of space in a medium or large kitchen. Left: A peninsular layout provides extra storage and preparation space, effectively separating the work zone from the dining area.

Right: When planning a kitchen, at least 1200mm should be allowed between units that are opposite each other. The levels of the worktop and units should also be taken into account; recommended heights for average-sized adults are shown here. Far right: A tall unit such as an oven housing unit should be placed at the end of a run of units so that it doesn't interrupt the worktop, and the hob should not be immediately adjacent to it.

Fitting heights

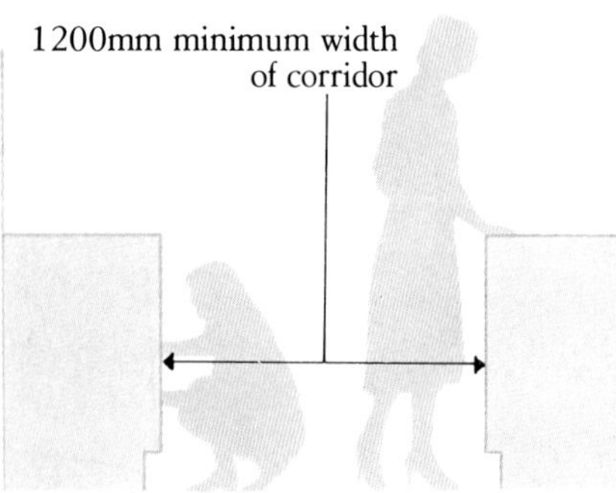

Fitting heights (from floor)
(recommended for persons of average size)

Work surfaces—including cooker	850mm to 1000mm
Sink top	900mm to 1050mm
Bottom of wall units above worktop	1350mm
Top of highest unit	1950mm to 2250mm
Highest shelf for general use	1750mm
Minimum floor space between walls of fittings	1200mm

ideal height is 50mm below your bent elbow when you are standing at it. Also, remember that a toe space about 100mm deep and 75mm high must be allowed along the bottom of the base units so you can stand close up to them comfortably and without stubbing your toes.

Other useful guidelines when you are planning vertically are that wall units or shelves should be hung at least 400mm above the worktop—any lower and the space at the back of the worktop would be inaccessible. The worktop itself should also project by about 300mm in front of the wall unit.

Most of the storage space will be above and below the work surface, but bending and stretching are tiring so try to keep everything you use regularly within easy reach—no lower than 750mm from the floor and no higher than 1750mm. Recommended fitting heights from the floor are shown on the left.

Picturing your kitchen

Now that you have some idea of the basic principles of kitchen planning, next comes the tricky part: adapting one of the text-book layouts to fit the shape and size of your kitchen.

The best way to go about this is to draw out your ideas on paper. You don't need to be an artist; and you need no special equipment, just some plain paper, graph paper, sharp pencils, a ruler, a rubber, a retractable steel rule, stiff paper and some scissors.

To get an all-round picture of the kitchen you'll have to make five accurate drawings: one of the floor plan and one each of the four walls.

First make rough sketches of each, marking in the fixed features such as doors, windows, drains, alcoves, boilers, radiators or a hatch.

Next, using the steel rule, fill in all the measurements in metric. Measure the overall height and width of the room as well as the distances between fixtures. Rooms are rarely perfectly straight so where you are measuring horizontal distances, say between a door and the corner of the room, measure twice, once just above the skirting board and once 900mm up from the floor. If there is any discrepancy between the two, take the smaller as the working size. Calculate vertical dimensions, for example from the floor to the lower edge of a window frame, using the same method.

When the rough sketches are fully labelled with measurements, use them to make accurate scale drawings on the graph paper. Work to a ratio that is practical and that you find easy to relate to, such as one small square:100mm or one large square:200mm.

Now indicate the exact positions of all fixed features, the sites of the water supply and drainage, existing gas and electrical points, the swing arcs of the doors and, if you know them, the routes of any chased-in wiring or pipework.

It is also a good idea at this stage to mark the positions of fixtures on the outside of the walls, such as downpipes or balconies, as some of the improvements you are planning may conflict with them.

When you draw out the plans, check and re-check the measurements and positions. Accuracy is crucial to a fitted kitchen.

Next, from stiff paper, make shapes representing all the equipment and units you are keeping or intend buying; these should be to the same scale as your plan. Cut out the shapes and label them, indicating their height and the hinge-side of any door they may have. Arrange the shapes on the floor plan, moving them around until you find a workable layout.

Important factors

If you don't know where to start, work on the assumption that you are unlikely to move the plumbing—it is expensive and inconvenient to change—and site the sink near the existing water supply and waste. This gives you the centre point of your triangle around which to build.

There are other factors, too, that may dictate the layout. A hob or cooker shouldn't be positioned under a window, in a corner, at the end of a run of units or next to a door. Allow for a heatproof surface either side for resting pans as they come off the hob.

Don't hang wall units directly over a hob, where they could be scorched or their contents affected by heat or steam. (You can, however, combine a small wall

Above: This photograph shows the bird's eye viewpoint you'll need to imagine when drawing up plans of your kitchen. (To see what this kitchen looks like from a more conventional angle, turn to page 23.)

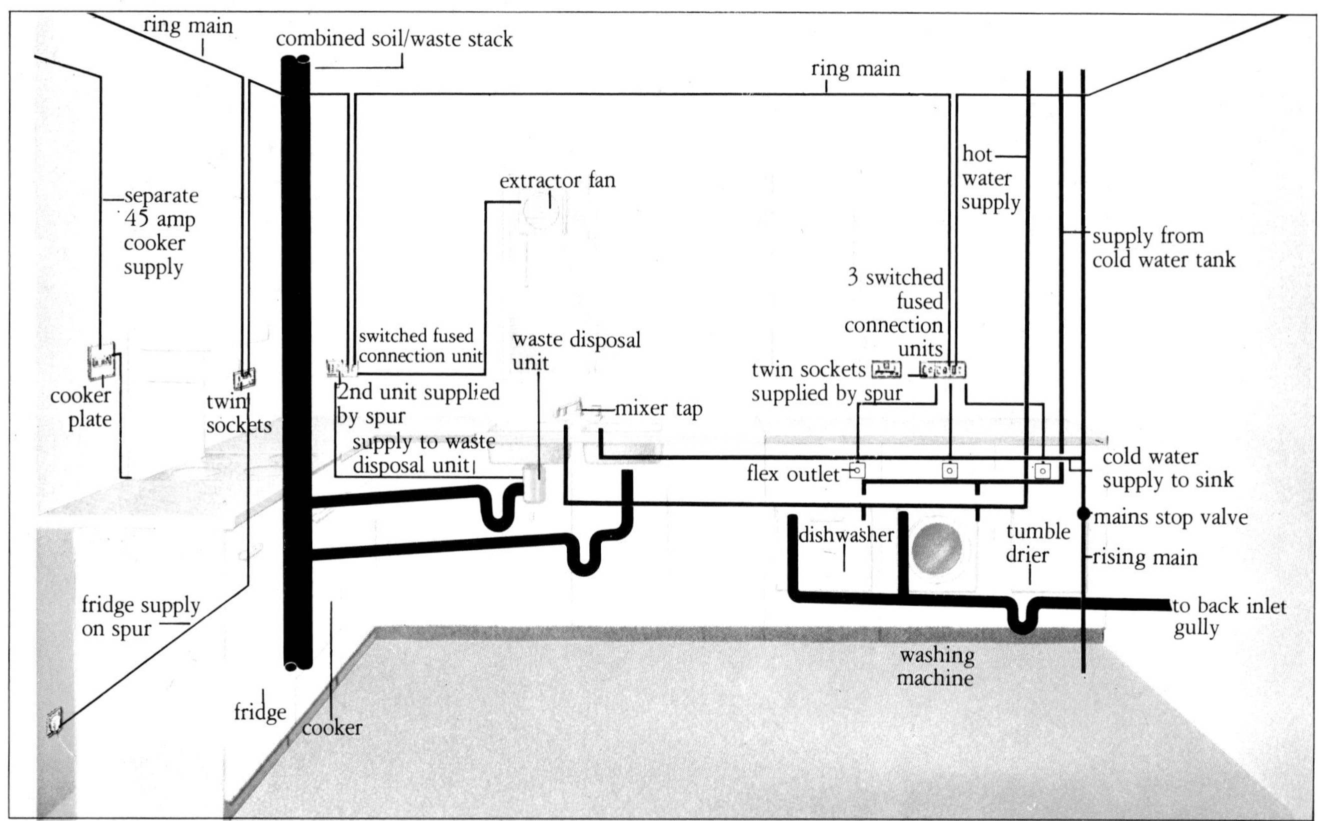

Above: The existing plumbing and wiring, and any adaptations that will be necessary, must be taken into account when planning a new kitchen. There should be sufficient sockets, none of them too near the sink. The dishwasher, washing machine and sink all need to be near the hot and cold water supplies and also drainage. Here the fridge has been placed next to the cooker, which is not a good idea, as it has to work overtime whenever the oven is used. Facing page: A cooker hood above a hob that is not on an outside wall will either need to be the re-circulating type or have to be ducted to an outside wall if it is an extractor hood.

unit with a cooker hood, which is useful if you want a complete run of units.) Try to place the hob or cooker on an outside wall so any cooker hood can discharge the fumes straight out of the house; otherwise you'll have to duct the fumes to an outside wall, or have a recirculating hood instead.

Don't interrupt a span of work surface with a tall unit. High-level ovens, fridge-freezers, stacked laundry equipment and broom cupboards should all be placed at the end of a run. Also, hobs and sinks should be at least 400mm away from a tall unit.

Try not to place the fridge or freezer side by side with the oven, or it will have to work overtime to compensate.

Don't position a sink in a corner, where it will be awkward to use. If you don't have a dishwasher, allow for a draining board on both sides of the sink.

Note which way doors of units and equipment open and avoid clashes. Sometimes doors can be reversed to open at the other side—if you want equipment such as a fridge or cooker with non-standard opening, check before you buy that it can be done and persuade the supplier to do it for you. Although many manufacturers claim that reversing a door is a diy job, it is not always simple, and any disasters that happen when you try may not be covered by the guarantee.

Make sure all wall units have base units, appliances or a table under them.

Fundamental alterations

If, despite your best efforts, you can't make a satisfactory work triangle take shape, think about changing the kitchen. Badly positioned doors and windows can be moved, and so can radiators and gas and electrical supplies. Non load-bearing walls can be taken down. Although the extra work involved will add to the cost of the job, it may not be by as much as you think; and the benefits to be gained could outweigh all but the most pressing financial considerations.

Not all changes need be costly or complicated. For example, a door which opens into the room taking up valuable floor space could be re-hung to open outwards. Alternatively, it could be replaced with a folding, sliding or saloon door, or even removed all together and replaced with a bead or fabric curtain.

Some of the improvements you are contemplating are likely to be affected by building regulations. These vary according to the kind of house you live in, so before you go ahead, check that your ideas meet with official approval.

Plumbing and electrics

During the planning stage, make sure that the services—water, drainage, gas and electricity—will be adequate. Apart from the sink, the dishwasher and washing machine will need water and drainage. If you don't possess either of these machines at the moment but hope to buy them later, have the necessary pipework made ready now—it will save you trouble and expense in the long run.

Install gas points and separate fused sockets for the hob and oven or the cooker. Even if you favour one fuel over another, provide supplies for both, as your choice of equipment may change in the future, and when you sell the house the purchaser may not share your preferences. Running new pipes or wiring in an already fitted kitchen causes certain disruption.

Electrical sockets must be planned into the layout at this stage, too. Having worked out what equipment you will use at each point in the work triangle, it will be easier to decide where the sockets are needed. You should have a minimum of four double-switched sockets, and more if you use or are likely to use a lot of electrical equipment. Estimate the number on the precept that you will *never* use an adaptor in the kitchen.

If you are having the kitchen rewired, install only double sockets. They cost marginally more than single ones but a lot less than having extra sockets added in the future. To save you bending and to keep them away from children's inquisitive fingers, position the sockets on the wall about 20–25cm above the worktop, and at a safe distance from the sink.

Safety first

The kitchen is potentially the most dangerous room in the house, but safety measures built in at the planning stage can prevent it from being an accident black spot.

Avoid putting the cooker in a corner or near a window, where a breeze could extinguish the gas flame or blow curtains over the heat source. Don't put it near a door either, as someone going out or coming in could knock against the cooker or the pans. Keep a fire extinguisher or fire blanket close to the cooker. Choose a floor covering that is smooth, easy to clean and non-slip, and repair or replace it when it shows signs of wear.

If there are children around, provide child-proof catches on cupboards, use a guard round the top of the cooker or hob and protect electrical sockets with special shields. For young children make a play area away from, but within sight of, the

Above and facing page: Good lighting is very important in a kitchen. Tracks of spotlights (above) are useful because the light can be directed exactly where it is needed, for example on to the worktops or into some cupboards. A pendant light (far right) should only be used in the eating area.

busy cooking zone; that way you can keep an eye on them without the children or their toys becoming a hazard.

Pets who sleep or are fed in the kitchen should be allocated their own place away from the food preparation area.

When the new kitchen is finished, make safety a routine. Store the things you want every day in a handy place, reserving high shelves for the things you seldom use. When you do need to reach high-level storage, use proper kitchen steps or a step-stool, not a chair.

Keep sharp, hot and poisonous things, including cleaning materials, in a safe place and out of reach of children.

Be tidy: clutter on the work surface and on the floor can cause accidents by camouflaging dangerous equipment, tripping you up or providing a suitable breeding ground for germs. Mop up spills straightaway—they make even the safest floor slippery.

Keep cupboard doors shut. Youngsters can crash into open base unit doors, and wall unit doors left ajar can give you a nasty blow on the head or face.

Turn pan handles and kettle spouts inwards; they are a temptation to children and easily caught in loose sleeves or gaping pockets when you walk past. Don't let electrical flexes trail, especially when they're near water or a heat source, and don't let steam pour on to an electrical socket.

Making light work

Good lighting is essential to safety, so design it carefully. It must fulfil three roles. For general all-over illumination, it should be clear and glare-free. For working, it needs to be bright and direct, and for eating or relaxing, flexible and controllable.

Natural light is the most valuable for overall light, as in many homes the room is used mainly during the day. Make sure the windows are not obstructed by elaborate curtains—in a kitchen, a blind is often best—or on the outside by vigorously growing plants.

For artificial general light, you'll need a ceiling fitting; the choice is between fluorescent and tungsten. Fluorescent tubes are cool-burning, long-lasting and cheap to run, and they provide bright, almost shadowless light. However, some people find that the almost indiscernible flickering, which is characteristic, causes headaches, and the cold light tends to distort colours making food look unappetizing. To reduce this effect choose a coloured fluorescent tube—for kitchens, deluxe warm white is the best.

Tungsten bulbs have a shorter life, but their warm, mellow light is very pleasant to live with. Available in almost every shape and size, they can be used in a variety of fittings. Track-mounted spotlights are useful because their beam can be directed precisely where it is wanted and adjusted when needs change. Downlighters, which are recessed in the ceiling, give a clean widespread wash of light, minimizing shadows.

A good working light can be provided by fluorescent or tungsten tubes fitted under the front edge of wall units and protected by lipping to save your eyes from glare and the tube from being knocked.

More intense light for special preparation areas like the hob or sink can come from strategically placed spotlights. A cooker hood above the hob will also provide localized light.

Gloomy cupboards and alcove shelving can be lit by concealed fluorescent tubes to dramatic effect. In the case of cupboards, the light can be operated by a door switch so it comes on automatically when the cupboard is opened.

Pendant lights are best reserved for 'mood' lighting over a dining table. A dimmer switch will help you control the level of light exactly. Rise-and-fall fittings are particularly good over a table which will be used for activities other than eating, as the lamp can be raised up out of the way.

For maximum flexibility, the three different kinds of lighting should be separately switched so that they can each be used independently.

CHAPTER 3

Inside story

In the kitchen, storage and space saving are two problems that go hand in hand. Overcome the first and you are well on the way to solving the second.

When you consider that the primary function of most kitchen furniture and fittings is to provide a home for food and equipment, it becomes clear that by condensing and rationalizing storage, you can make much better use of the available space.

Rationalization policy

One obvious way to cut the amount of storage you need is to reduce the number of things you store. You can do this by appraising everything in the kitchen and then finding a new home for those things not directly to do with food; by relocating cooking equipment you rarely use to less accessible cupboards; and by ruthlessly getting rid of redundant items you seldom or never use.

Among the things that need not, or should not, be kept in the kitchen are household and shoe-cleaning materials; garden tools, fertilizers, pesticides and weed killers; and the diy kit. All would be better and more safely stowed away in an under-stairs cupboard or garden shed. Laundry equipment, as already mentioned, should, if possible, be moved to a utility room, bathroom or garage.

If you have a separate dining room or dining area and only take breakfast and snack meals in the kitchen, most of the china, glass and cutlery and all the linen apart from tea towels can be kept there, where it will be conveniently placed for laying the table.

Equipment that is used only occasionally can be put right away when it is not wanted. The under-stairs cupboard, garage, cellar and loft are all useful for long-term storage, but try to match their accessibility to the frequency with which you will need the things you keep there.

Seasonal cookware tends to be on a large scale: turkey roasting tins, preserving pans, Christmas cake tins, winemaking kit, picnic baskets and so on. But as it comes into its own only once a year or so, you can wrap it up and pack it away in the attic along with the Christmas decorations, thus leaving tracts of shelf and cupboard space clear.

Things needed more frequently, but not every day, such as spare glasses and dishes for parties, a barbecue or a fish kettle, can be kept handy in a utility room or cupboard where they are easily reached when wanted but don't take up precious kitchen space.

Throwing things away is probably the most difficult form of rationalization. Most of us have a collection of kitchen gadgets we no longer use but can't bear to part with, either because they were given by friends who would be hurt to know they'd been passed on to a jumble sale or because there's always a chance they'll be useful one day. Harden your heart and take stock: anything you haven't used for two years is unlikely ever to be an asset to your kitchen, so get rid of it.

Fitted kitchens

Having whittled down your batterie de cuisine, you must now decide on a convenient way to keep it. The most popular approach to general storage is the fitted kitchen, which slots the maximum

Below: It's hard to beat a fitted kitchen for neat, easy-to-clean, efficient storage and work surfaces.

Above left: A pull-out trolley is just one of the clever ways that kitchen units can be adapted to individual requirements. Above right: Special fittings to organize the insides of kitchen cabinets include a wide variety of items such as cutlery trays and bread boxes.

amount of cupboard space around the principal pieces of equipment.

Fitted kitchens are composed of units which can be made to measure and installed by a kitchen specialist or local carpenter; or pre-built to certain standard specifications, and then either installed by professional fitters, or flat-packed ready for self-assembly by the customer. Prices vary according to the design, quality, flexibility and method of fitting.

Whichever type you fancy, before you buy, go and see the units in a proper kitchen setting—either in a showroom or, if you want a tailor-made kitchen, in someone's home. Any reputable installer will be happy to give you the names of satisfied customers who can vouch for his proficiency. Brochures will give you an idea of what the finished kitchen will look like, but the only way to check for quality is to see the real thing. Most kitchen suppliers appreciate the importance of this, so much so that diy supermarkets now also have kitchen settings to show their self-assembly ranges.

Construction

Both ready-manufactured and self-assembly kitchens are made up of the carcass (sides, base and sometimes back of the unit with basic shelves and the body of the drawer), doors and drawer fronts, and a worktop.

The carcass is usually made from some comparatively cheap board, which is either laminated or painted to give it a white or sand-coloured easy-clean surface.

The doors and drawer fronts come in a vast range of styles, colours, textures and finishes—these are what give the kitchen its character. Some have reversible door panels with a different colour or finish on each side so you can ring the changes.

Solid wood in natural tones is especially popular, as it is warm and cozy-looking and very sturdy; it is also quite expensive. Wood veneer is less dear and very similar in effect. Both solid wood and wood veneer are treated to make them water- and steam-resistant.

The principal alternative to wood is laminate, which is easy to clean, durable and not too expensive. It comes in a wide choice of colours, and textured as well as smooth finishes. Some laminate ranges are trimmed with wood.

At the expensive end of the market

are new, very attractive finishes like lacquered resin or polyester, varnished rattan or bamboo, and hand-painted wood using specialist techniques like rag-rolling, hand-dragging, stippling or sponging.

The work surfaces, too, can be made from a variety of materials, including wood, plastics, tiles, stainless steel and, most commonly, laminate. Again, a wide range of colours and a choice of textures are available.

Although unit ranges are designed with colour co-ordination in mind, manufacturers usually leave you to choose the combination of door finish and worktop you prefer, which gives you a little scope for originality.

Dimensions

Unit sizes are standard, with base units most commonly 900mm high (though 850mm high base units are also available) and 600mm deep (but 500mm deep units are also available). Widths of base units are generally 300, 400, 500, 600, 800, 1,000, 1,200, 1,500 and 1,800mm. Wall units are usually either 600 or 900mm high (though there are smaller ones, about 300mm high, for use with cooker hoods and above tall units). The widths correspond to base unit widths. Housing units for ovens and refrigerators are between 2,000 and 2,250mm high.

Unit sizes were standardized to correspond to the dimensions of built-in appliances, so the depth and height measurements are pretty well fixed. There is more flexibility in the widths, however, with the more expensive kitchens offering a range of sizes and the cheapest ones three or four.

In the middle to upper price ranges, where it is difficult to fit standard units into the given space, manufacturers will sometimes make up special sizes.

Left: A carousel unit is a useful accessory for a corner cupboard. Below: Self-assembly units can look just as smart as ready-manufactured ranges.

Below and right: The efficiency of base units can be increased by installing items like a lift-up work surface, corner carousels, a slide-out ironing board and wire baskets.

What to look for

Apart from making sure the units you want come in the right colour and range of sizes, check that they are well built. Cupboards should be rigid with well made joints and square corners. Note whether or not they have a solid back—open-backed units are more vulnerable to dust and dirt which can creep up from the floor behind.

Surfaces should be sound. If they get scratched or chipped in the showroom, will they stand up to everyday life in your kitchen? Do the doors and drawers show every finger mark? If they do, you could be buying yourself a full-time cleaning job.

The doors should open easily and close firmly and quietly without bouncing open again. There should be no sharp edges, and the handles or knobs should be easy to grasp without breaking your fingernails or grazing your knuckles. The inside must be easy to clean, preferably with removable drawer linings that can be washed in the sink. Avoid joins and ledges that will trap dirt; rounded edges are easier to keep clean.

On an aesthetic level, make sure your choice includes all the refinements you would like such as decorative shelves, glass-fronted cupboards or décor panels. Most display areas are too small to include every variation in the range, so if you don't see what you want in the sample kitchen, ask.

Units are first and foremost for storage, so make sure they do the job well. Shelves must be adjustable; you'll be storing things of different heights, so to make maximum use of the space you'll need deep shelves for tall packages and shallow ones for short things.

Most kitchens offer a range of fittings to organize space more efficiently. Wire vegetable drawers, pull-out larder units, deep drawers for pans, integral bread bins, slide-out ironing boards, breakfast bars and mixer housings are just a few of the devices available.

These purpose-made fittings are very useful but don't be tempted to organize your storage down to the last teaspoon—your needs are bound to change, so allow scope for flexibility.

Self-assembly kitchens

The choice between self-assembly and ready-manufactured kitchens is largely one of cost these days: self-assembly are almost always less expensive. Once in place, they are virtually indistinguishable from professionally installed units.

As with ready-manufactured units, there is a range of colours, materials (including solid wood and laminates), sizes, fittings and prices available.

Generally speaking, assembling the units is not difficult—they are designed with the amateur in mind and do not usually require special tools. Nevertheless, you should check beforehand that the particular range you have in mind will not be beyond your capabilities to install. Bear in mind that it's often the kitchen, not the units, that presents the problems—for instance, a floor may not be quite level or walls absolutely straight.

If you have any doubts, about your capabilities, enlist the aid of a handy friend or call in hired help. Some self-assembly manufacturers will install them for you for an additional charge.

Another point to remember if you are doing more than just adding on a few units is that a kitchen needs water, drainage, gas and electricity, and unless you know what you are doing, plumbing and electrical work ought to be left to the professionals. Gas connections should never be made by anyone other than a qualified fitter.

Alternative storage

If you don't want to invest in a fitted kitchen, alternative general storage can be provided, very attractively, by free-standing furniture. A traditional dresser combines plenty of shelf space, cupboards and drawers in one good-looking piece of furniture. Corner cupboards, sideboards, chest of drawers and even old school-room cupboards can also be pressed into service. If your kitchen is big enough, a large Victorian wardrobe or linen press, suitably converted inside with extra shelves, makes a practical and handsome store for tinned and packaged food, drinks, glass, china, cutlery, serving dishes and linen.

Shelves are the simplest and most versatile form of storage. Fix one at picture rail level to run all round the room, above the doors and windows, and you have the perfect out-of-the-way place to keep seldom used equipment.

Make narrow shelves deep enough to take just one row of jars and hang them on the wall just above the worktop, where they'll keep cooking ingredients and seasonings within easy reach while you cook (though, strictly speaking, herbs and spices ought to be stored in a cool, dark place).

Below left: Self-assembly kitchens are the modern compromise between the expense of custom-built units and the complexities of making your own.
Below right: A narrow shelf on the wall immediately above the worktop turns an often unused area into handy storage space.

Shelves fitted in alcoves make good use of otherwise 'dead' space, and if you fix roller blinds in front of them, their contents can be hidden from view when you're not using them. In this situation, system shelving, where brackets are slotted into metal uprights attached to the wall, is more adaptable than fixed shelves, as the height of the shelves can be changed when necessary. If you already have fixed shelves, one way of making better use of the space between them is to suspend wire baskets from them to hang underneath.

The main disadvantages of shelf storage are that things get dusty and, unless you are very tidy, into a terrible muddle. Organize the space by decanting dried foods into matching jars. A row of neatly labelled, gleaming glass containers is far easier to keep clean and looks much better than a jumble of half-used packets.

Small-scale storage

Shallow baskets are useful for keeping utensils, tea towels and the inevitable collection of paper, pencils, string and so on in some semblance of order. Wire or natural baskets are good for fruit and vegetables, pottery crocks for bread and flour, and colourful plastic crates for cleaning materials. A pair of book ends keeps cookery tomes in their place.

Some of the things you keep in the kitchen need special storage arrangements. Sharp kitchen knives, for example, must be put in a safe place but they must also be handy when needed. A wall-mounted magnetic rack fixed between the worktop and wall unit keeps them in full view so the blades won't be grasped accidentally; a slot cut in the back of the worktop holds them, blade down, out of the reach of children. A knife block—a huge chunk of wood with slots for protecting the blades—does a similar job but is portable.

Cooking utensils are awkwardly shaped and difficult to store in drawers. Hang them on a wall-mounted rack (some sets of tools come with their own), stand them in a jar or purpose-made revolving carousel, or hang them from a wall grid using little hooks. Larger utensils and pans can be stored above eye level but within arm's reach by hanging them on butcher's hooks from a wood or metal pole which itself is suspended from the ceiling.

Rolls of greaseproof paper, foil and cling film need to be stored in a special dispenser. According to how often you need them, the dispenser may be fixed to the inside of a cupboard door—the shelves being made shallower to accommodate it—to the wall above the work top or to the side of a wall unit. The roll-holder for kitchen paper can be fixed to the underside of a wall unit.

Storing food is fairly straightforward, but do remember that ultimately all packaged food is perishable. If it does not actually go bad, it can become infested with weevils or, at the very least, lose its flavour. Mark everything you buy with the date, and check regularly that no packets are lurking forgotten at the back of a cupboard. Small packets and jars are often overlooked and should be kept at the front of the cupboard or stored on a special wire rack fixed to the back of the cupboard door where the contents can be seen at a glance.

China needs quite a lot of storage space, but if you have dishes that are in daily use, you can save cupboard space by making the draining rack their permanent home. Fix the rack to the wall over the draining board so as not to take up worktop space. If you like an uncluttered kitchen, you could build a bottomless cupboard around it, so that when the doors are closed the plates can drip-dry unseen behind them.

Facing page (left and right): Simple, open shelving looks informal and rustic and makes good use of alcoves; even an old fireplace can be utilized this way. Left above: Learn to make maximum use of wall space. Utensils can be hung from hooks or a rack, vegetables kept in hanging baskets, knives stored on a wall-mounted magnetic rack, and plates put straight into a plate rack after being washed. Left below: Open shelves painted or stained to match base units make a pretty display as well as providing storage space, and are much less expensive than wall units.

Above: Little-used space can make a good place for a wine rack to store all kinds of bottles.

Glass needs no special storage treatment except that it should stand right way up to avoid damaging the rim, which is the most vulnerable part.

Wine racks make useful storage for bottles of all kinds. They are available as separate racks, to tuck away on a low shelf or hang on a wall, or they can sometimes be built-in to a fitted kitchen. However, handy though it is to store wine in the kitchen, a cool, dark area is really more suitable.

Trays, chopping boards and pastry slabs take up less space and are more easily accessible if you store them on end. A gap between units, partitioned vertically, makes the perfect rack for all these things. Alternatively, if your units fit so neatly into the available space that there are no suitable gaps, you could partition off part of the inside of a cupboard to store these items upright.

A safe, hygienic place must be found for the rubbish bin. Many kitchen units come with a lidded bucket fitted to the back of the sink unit door. When the door is opened, the lid lifts automatically so you need not touch it when you're handling food. Another clever—but custom-made—idea for disposing of rubbish is to cut an opening in the worktop in the food preparation area and cover it with a hinged lid which is also a chopping board. The bin is kept in the cupboard beneath the opening, so after vegetables have been prepared on the chopping board it can be lifted and the peelings swept down into the bin below.

Dead areas

Apart from making best use of existing storage, you can save space simply by being inventive and never letting a single cubic centimetre go to waste.

In fitted kitchens there are two notorious 'dead' areas: the corners, and the space behind the plinths.

The plinth space may seem too small to worry about but it is very useful and some kitchen manufacturers now make plinth drawers to hold things you would rather not keep together with food and cooking equipment, such as shoe cleaning things, a tool kit and even a nifty fold-away pair of steps. If the range of units you have chosen does not offer these useful space-savers, any reasonably adept handyman should be able to make them up for you.

Kitchen manufacturers have also tackled the problem of inaccessible corner space and come up with a couple of solutions: revolving shelves and double-hinged doors.

Revolving shelves are half-circular trays of plastic, coated wire or metal which swing out as the cupboard door opens. They are fine for carrying evenly spread loads of medium to light-weight items. But under heavy loads, the shelves (especially of the plastic and wire

Left: Built-in units can be adapted to fit any space by utilizing narrow cupboards, wine racks and display shelves. Above: A double-hinged door and carousel make the best use of an awkward corner.

systems) may distort, affecting the revolving action.

Double-hinged doors are hinged at the side and again at the centre to fit right round a corner. When the cupboard is open, the whole of the shelf area is visible and accessible although you may have to stretch to reach anything at the back.

As kitchens are not normally divisible into neat unit widths, there are bound to be gaps between the units. These can be used to store trays, house a telescopic towel rail, provide space for folding steps or a stool or, in the hands of a clever carpenter, become a vertical wine rack or accommodate narrow slide-out storage baskets.

The ends of units are seldom used, but they can be a wonderful place to put extra shelves or wall-mounted gadgets, racks or pin boards. Where wall units flank a window, small shelves fixed to the sides get the benefit of maximum daylight and become a marvellous place to grow herbs. The ends of base units can accommodate a rail for a hand towel or hooks from which to hang saucepans.

In a kitchen where there's no room to serve meals, a folding table might ease the space situation. Opening out into floor area normally used as a traffic route, the table then folds flat against the wall taking up next to no space. To go with it, choose slim, folding chairs which can hang from hooks on the wall when not in use, leaving the floor quite clear.

CHAPTER 4

On the surface

Kitchen surfaces—walls, floors, worktops, even the ceiling, doors and windows—have to be tough. But being washable and durable no longer has to also mean dull.

Once you've decided on the kitchen's structure, its layout and main fixtures, you need to put it into context. And that means thinking about surfaces. The walls, floors, worktops and windows are the obvious areas for consideration, but don't forget about the ceiling and doors as they have an important part to play, too. Together with the units or furniture, the surfaces will be among the major factors influencing the style and ambiance of the room as well as its convenience and practicality.

Don't underestimate the importance of getting the décor right—any working environment should be sympathetic and the kitchen is no exception. But while you choose colours, textures and patterns based on your own personal taste and the atmosphere you want to create (and there's more about this in Chapter Six), you must harden your heart against unsuitable materials and consider only those that will stand up to kitchen life.

Above: Every surface in the kitchen can be part of an overall décor scheme. Here a wood-panelled ceiling and a plain laminated worktop with wood lipping complement the striking tiles used for the floor and splashback.

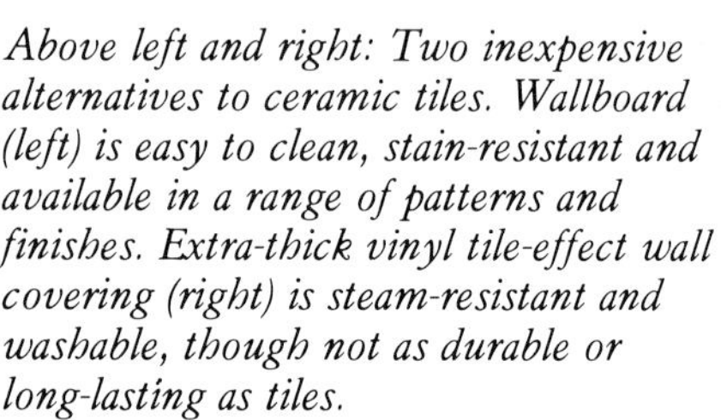

Above left and right: Two inexpensive alternatives to ceramic tiles. Wallboard (left) is easy to clean, stain-resistant and available in a range of patterns and finishes. Extra-thick vinyl tile-effect wall covering (right) is steam-resistant and washable, though not as durable or long-lasting as tiles.

Wall coverings

Before you deal with the walls, make sure they are dry and in good condition. Crumbling plaster won't hold any of the gadgets you want to hang up, and penetrating damp will ruin decorations in no time. Dampness caused by condensation can be relieved by using warm-to-the-touch wall coverings, but it is only eliminated by improved heating and ventilation.

When you come to choose a wall covering or surface treatment, it's important to opt for one that is washable, hard-wearing and resistant to a certain amount of heat and damp.

In a fitted kitchen the wall is divided into two separate areas: the space between the worktop and wall units, and the surface above the units and on walls where there is no work area at all. As these areas receive different wear, the materials used can be different as well.

The wall directly above the worktop is sometimes known as the splashback, for obvious reasons. Its proximity to food preparation and all the activity which that entails means that it will be knocked, splashed and spattered with food and sometimes exposed to heat from the hob, so it must be covered with a heavy-duty surface of some sort.

Tiles and other splashback coverings

Ceramic tiles are a popular choice as they can be wiped over quickly and easily. Stainless steel tiles have similar virtues and look effective in a modern kitchen. However, both kinds can be expensive and, once fixed, are semi-permanent.

Alternatives are plastic laminated panels or polyester-coated wallboards, which give a smooth, virtually seamless, washable surface; tongue-and-groove wood panelling, which looks attractive and can be varnished or painted to make it water resistant; or even vinyl floor tiles or sheet flooring which is extremely robust and gives you the opportunity to

Left: Cork's rich texture and natural warmth blend well with most décors. It is easy to put up and comes in a variety of patterns, but sealing is recommended to make the cork resistant to steam and moisture.

match the splashback to your flooring.

Wall area not adjacent to the worktop won't need such a durable surface, so here the choice lies between vinyl-coated wall covering, paint or a natural surface such as tongue-and-groove pine, bare brick or cork.

Vinyl wall-coverings and paint

If you want pattern, vinyl wall-covering is best as it offers an almost limitless variety of designs and colours to suit any style. Unless yours is a very large and well-ventilated kitchen, avoid ordinary uncoated wallpaper. As well as not being steam-resistant or washable, it will quickly discolour in the warm, sometimes smoky, atmosphere. Vinyl wall-covering also discolours in time but it will stay looking fresh longer, and is both steam resistant and washable.

Paint is a cheap, cheerful and easy way to decorate, and it comes in every colour you could possibly want. Use oil-based eggshell paint or vinyl silk emulsion, both of which are completely washable. Gloss paint is also tough and washable but its shiny surface may aggravate any existing condensation problem and, if the wall surface is less than perfect, its reflective properties will in certain lights show up every single blemish.

Wood, brick and cork

Natural wood is the perfect background for food and makes an attractive kitchen wall-covering. Tongue-and-groove boards have to be fixed on to a framework of battens which is first screwed to the wall. The resulting space between wall and boards makes it ideal for concealing poor plaster, surface-run pipework and many other imperfections. The gap also provides a certain amount of insulation against noise.

The boards are usually placed vertically but you could fix them horizontally to make a small kitchen seem larger, or diagonally or in chevrons for a more interesting effect.

Once fixed, the wood should be smoothed and coated with clear varnish or one of the semi-transparent coloured varnishes, which tint the wood without obscuring its grain.

Bare brick looks wonderfully wholesome and appeals to those with a romantic yearning for the country life. If you have good, sound walls with no pipework or wiring chased in to them (and do check this first) you can remove the plaster to expose the brick. The brickwork may need re-pointing and will certainly have to be coated with a clear masonry sealer to protect it.

Cork comes in tile, panel or roll form ready to be glued to the wall. It can be bought natural or ready-coated with a plastic finish. The natural surface is soft and slightly granular so it has poor resistance to dirt and impact. However, it is warm to the touch, has some sound insulation properties and contributes a lovely coziness to the room. It would be perfect for an eating area or in a little desk corner where it could double as a pin board. Plasticized cork is more practical, but the coating gives it an unnatural sheen, which is disconcerting for a wall-covering though perfectly acceptable for flooring.

Facing page: Plain ceramic tiles look good with natural wood units and are durable and easy to clean. Far left: Cork comes as tiles, rolls or panels. Think about the effect you are after before making your final choice. Dark, chunky tiles (top of picture) are best used sparingly—for example on a feature wall as a contrast to melamine cupboards. Sheet cork in rolls (centre of picture) is ideal for walls with a lot of doors, cupboards or windows, where using tiles might involve too much fiddly cutting. Flecked tiles (bottom right of picture) are great if you want the cork to harmonize with an existing colour scheme, or you could choose natural flecking (top left of picture) for a more neutral effect. The soft tones of plain cork tiles (bottom left of picture) go with just about any decorative scheme. Left: Quarry tiles are enjoying a new lease of life thanks to their natural looks and hard-wearing reliability. The colours—brick red, buffs, browns and blue-greys—and the unglazed finish give them a rustic look that teams well with today's modern furnishings. Quarry tiles come in a range of shapes and sizes.

Floor coverings

The floor is probably the largest uninterrupted area in the room, so think hard about the colour and design of its covering. It should be in keeping with the units and reinforce the style you have set out to create. It should also, of course, be practical: smooth, level and non-slip for safety, tough, easy to clean and comfortable underfoot. Again, the alternatives are synthetic or natural, modern or traditional.

Vinyl

Vinyl is perhaps the most practical and versatile of all kitchen floor coverings and is, therefore, popular and widely available in a good choice of designs. It comes in both sheet and tile form and can be laid on to solid or hardboarded timber floors.

Sheet vinyl comes in widths of up to four metres so it can provide a continuous, seamless surface in all but the very largest kitchens. It is usually cushioned to be easy on the feet and to provide a comfortable surface for children to play on.

Vinyl tiles are not seamless and are seldom cushioned but, like sheet flooring, they provide a hard-wearing, water- and grease-resistant surface. And, if you have an awkwardly shaped floor area, they may be more economical to lay than sheet vinyl.

Both sheet vinyl and tiles come in a vast range of colours, patterns, qualities and prices, and often laying them is a fairly simple diy job. The one disadvantage of vinyl is that it is not heat-resistant, and a dropped cigarette, red-hot pan from the hob, or ash from a solid fuel stove or boiler could do irreparable damage.

Ceramic floor tiles

Ceramic tiles are a traditional choice.

Right: Wooden worktops look beautiful, but they are expensive and require regular maintenance. Here they echo the panelled ceiling and wood trim of the units.

The mellow colours or ethnic patterns of quarry and terracotta, together with their characteristic irregularities, give them a rustic charm, while the uniform plain colours or sophisticated designs of glazed ceramic tiles make them perfect for a glossier modern kitchen.

All are good looking, durable, heat-resistant and easy to clean, and those who have them happily disregard their drawbacks—which are that they are cold to the touch, hard on the feet and rather expensive. As they are so heavy, they are best used at ground level and laid on a solid floor; atmospheric changes can make timber floors move slightly, which would cause the tiles to part or crack. Cutting tiles and laying them to form a perfectly smooth, level surface is a job for the professional or a very skilful and painstaking amateur.

Wood floors

As long as it is well sealed against water and dirt, wood makes a beautiful and practical kitchen floor—and if you sand down the existing boards and varnish them yourself, a fairly cheap one, too. The natural honey colour of the wood looks rich and warm, but unless the boards fit together snugly, it will be unpleasantly draughty. Depending on their width, gaps can be filled with slivers of wood or papier mâché tinted to match the boards.

If you like the look of wood but have a floor that is too poor to leave exposed, you could cover it with chipboard. This comes in tile or sheet form and is screwed or nailed down and then sealed like wood. The result is a lovely toffee-coloured finish that looks a bit like cork.

Cork flooring

Real cork is often used as a kitchen floor covering, as it is warm and easy to live with. Available in a range of natural

colours from light gold to dark peat, it comes in tile form and is much denser than the kind used for walls. You can buy it in its natural state, or sealed or vinyl coated. Natural cork is cheaper but extremely porous, so it must be sealed before it is walked on. Once laid, cork is as easy to look after as vinyl.

Kitchen carpets

Carpet may seem an unlikely floor covering for a room where cleanliness is essential, but some synthetic low-pile ones are made specially for the purpose. The main advantages are that it is soft, warm and quiet to walk on. Spills can be mopped or scraped up and the residue washed off very successfully, but general cleaning cannot be as thorough as for a smooth floor.

Worktops

The ideal worktop would resist heat, water, abrasive cleaners, household chemicals, kitchen knives and the impact of heavy pans; but unfortunately, the only materials that could stand up to all those things are the most expensive, like slate or granite. That is not to say that the alternatives do not do their job well—they do, but to get the best out of them you must respect their limitations.

Laminates

Plastic laminate, of which the best known is Formica, is the most popular material for worktops. It comes in many colours and patterns, ranging from floral and geometric through to natural look-alikes such as wood, cork, stone, leather, marble, granite or tile mosaic. The surface can be perfectly smooth or slightly textured, with some heavily studded or cross-hatched designs now available to suit hi-tech kitchens.

Laminated worktops come in continuous lengths of up to 3.60m, so dirt

Right: Tiles are becoming increasingly popular for worktops, and they are quick and easy to lay. Matt or unglazed tiles are preferable to heavily glazed ones, and there are special worktop tiles designed specifically for this area. Coloured grouting can be used to match the décor, but it must be a waterproof, non-toxic epoxy grout so it will resist water, dirt and germs.

collecting joins can be kept to a minimum. The edges may be either square, or post-formed with a rounded front edge and curved upturn at the back to stop spills from leaking down behind or crumbs from collecting between work-top and wall. Square edges are sometimes trimmed with wooden lipping.

Laminates are resistant to water, reasonable impact and most household chemicals and cleaners. They can, however, stain and be damaged by heat and kitchen knife blades, so keep trivets and wooden chopping boards handy.

Ceramic tiles

Ceramic tiles make a handsome hard-wearing surface that resists water, heat and stains. Available in designs and patterns to go with every style of kitchen from farmhouse to city apartment, they can be continued up on to the wall to make an all-in-one surface and splash-back that helps visually increase the size of the kitchen, especially if it is narrow.

Ranges of tiles designed specifically for worktops include rounded edging tiles for the front and concave ones for the back. To make the worktop, the tiles are fixed on to a blockboard or chipboard counter-top and then grouted with epoxy grout, which is impervious to water.

It is the grouting lines that present the only real problem with tiles, as they collect dirt and so have to be scrubbed regularly and occasionally re-grouted.

As the surface is not smooth, you'll need a board for rolling out pastry. And although knife blades won't easily mark them, chopping straight on to tiles isn't very pleasant and won't do the knife much good either, so provide yourself with a chopping board.

Wood

Wooden worktops are in the luxury class, as they must be made from expensive hardwood. They look lovely, though, and will mellow with age, giving the kitchen an inimitable patina of maturity. Careful maintenance is essential, and surfaces should be cleaned and re-sealed regularly.

Chopping on wood leaves its mark, but as long as the same area is always used, it can add to its character. Hot pans straight from the hob will leave scorch marks and, in time, constant wetting will warp and split the wood around the sink, so both areas should be protected.

Corian and stainless steel

Corian is a comparatively new and miraculous plastic material used for making pastry boards and chopping boards, sinks and splashbacks as well as worktops. Resistant to stains, scratches, heat and water, it is smooth, with a translucent quality similar to marble. It comes in white and a number of soft off-white shades and can be custom-made to provide a seamless surface to fit along a whole run of units with an integral sink.

If you favour a hi-tech look, a stainless steel worktop is an option. It is easy to clean and resists practically everything except scratching. It will, however, show water marks if not wiped down after use. In a busy kitchen, it can be quite noisy and should be properly insulated underneath to reduce its resonance. Like Corian, it can be custom-made into complete worktops incorporating integral drainers and sinks and with a cut-out to accommodate the hob.

Compromises

Although no worktop is perfect, any of the ones mentioned could be modified to overcome its particular deficiency. A hardwood chopping board and a marble pastry slab let into the surface would take care of most food preparation tasks. A stainless steel or quarry tiled surface beside the hob would give a heatproof parking place for hot pans. And stainless

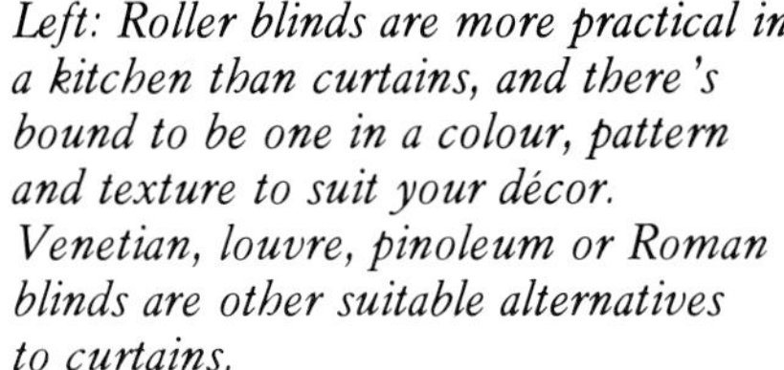

Left: Roller blinds are more practical in a kitchen than curtains, and there's bound to be one in a colour, pattern and texture to suit your décor. Venetian, louvre, pinoleum or Roman blinds are other suitable alternatives to curtains.

steel would protect the area around the sink from water damage.

Window treatments

The best kitchen window treatment is nothing at all. Bare windows allow the maximum daylight into the room, are easy to clean and could not be cheaper. However, if you are closely overlooked, or have an ugly view or a south-facing window that gets the full glare of the sun, you will need to dress it somehow.

Unless the window is right away from the working area, curtains are unsuitable—they collect grease and dirt from the atmosphere, harbour cooking smells and can be a fire hazard. If they are essential to the style of kitchen you want, however, then choose short ones in a washable material, and keep them tied back.

Blinds

Blinds will give privacy and protection from bright sun and can be just as decorative as curtains, but they are more practical. Depending on the size, shape and position of the window and your décor, choose from roller, venetian, vertical louvre, pinoleum or Roman blinds.

Roller blinds are neat, simple and widely available in many colours, patterns and textures. If you want a special motif at the window or to match a decorative feature in the room, you can have them specially printed with your own design. The roller mechanism can

Right: The most practical window treatment of all in a kitchen is to leave it bare, and if the window is particularly attractive, it's the nicest-looking method as well.

be spring- or cord-operated, and some of the new types have a neat plastic pelmet at the top to hide the working parts. Standard sizes can be bought off the peg, and in-between sizes made to measure. Roller blinds are best suited to narrow- and medium-width windows, as wider ones are sometimes difficult to operate smoothly.

Venetian blinds let in the light or shut it out at the pull of a cord. Most have slats made from plastic or painted metal, although wood slats, which look extremely handsome, are available if you seek them out. Narrow slats are the latest development in venetian blinds, making them look sharp and sleek—just right for a modern kitchen.

Vertical louvres are more suitable for large windows and patio doors as they can be drawn back like curtains. Their flexible slats come in a variety of colours and textures and will pivot to let in more or less light.

If you like natural materials, pinoleum blinds made from thin strips of wood are an attractive alternative. They are cord operated and roll up to open. For an altogether softer and more 'furnished' window treatment, Roman blinds might be the answer. Made from fabric, they hang as a straight panel when closed, pleating up into soft folds when open. You can sew them yourself from a kit, using any fabric you choose, or they can be professionally made.

Ceilings

Heat rises and, as it does, it takes particles of dust and grease with it, so in the kitchen, you need a ceiling that is easy to clean and won't show the dirt too readily.

Paint is easy to apply and to keep clean, especially if you use eggshell or vinyl silk. Choose white or a pale colour to reflect the maximum of light.

For a cozy atmosphere, or to visually reduce the height of the ceiling, you can paper it to match the walls. Again, use a washable surface such as vinyl wall-covering.

If you want to actually reduce the height of the room, or just cover up bad plaster, tongue-and-groove pine is good. Fix it close to the ceiling or on a framework suspended below it. The space between is particularly useful if you want to install downlighters.

Doors

The kitchen door must resist dirty finger-marks, scuffs and knocks. Gloss paint provides a perfectly tough surface that is wipe-clean and always comes up shining.

If you want something more interesting, you could cover a flush door with patterned pvc fabric, edging it with wood moulding painted or stained to match.

Where there are children, a door painted with blackboard paint makes a 'legal' graffiti site and might deter them from getting to work on more precious surfaces. Grown-ups will find a giant blackboard handy, too, for leaving messages, reminders and the shopping list.

But if such an expanse of black doesn't appeal, a large sheet of cork, left natural or covered with bright felt and fixed to cover the door, would make a good noticeboard.

Louvred doors have an airy Mediterranean look and, if you choose half-width ones, they can save space, too. Beware, though, of cooking smells permeating the rest of the house, and make sure kitchen ventilation is working efficiently.

If shortage of light is a problem, think about replacing solid doors with glass ones. If there is no frame, tinted or patterned glass is safest. But if you are just replacing the panels in a wooden door, stained, etched or wired glass will give it more character.

CHAPTER 5

All systems go

Equipping a kitchen can be a complex business, and the efficiency, convenience and appearance of the room all depend on the appliances you choose.

Well-designed, efficient equipment makes the cook's life much easier, so plan the machines you need into your kitchen scheme right at the start. If your budget won't allow you to buy everything you want straightaway, leave gaps so they can be added later.

The essentials which must take priority are the sink and taps, the cooker and the fridge. Depending on your lifestyle, you may or may not consider a freezer, dishwasher, waste disposer or cooker hood to be essential; but when resources are low, they can certainly come further down the list. Strictly speaking, laundry machines don't come under the heading of kitchen equipment at all, but as many households have no other place to put them, they may have to be incorporated.

Equipment in nearly all the categories mentioned comes in a variety of shapes, sizes and, often, colours in a wide range of prices. Nowadays, appliance manufacturers plan their equipment to blend into fitted kitchens unobtrusively. They can be tucked under worktops or built into housing units, with décor panels to camouflage them further if desired.

Always buy the best you can afford and choose models that will accommodate any possible future changes in the way you live. For example, if you are thinking of going back to work after a spell at home, an automatic washing machine will be more useful than a twin tub; and a large-size freezer and a cooker with an efficient auto-timer will solve many of the shopping and cooking problems.

If you have a small kitchen, there's a great temptation to go for small-size equipment, but do think carefully before you buy. The size of the equipment should relate to the number of people in the household and the workload, rather than to the available space.

Anything too small to do the job required quickly and efficiently will become a constant source of irritation no matter how much elbow room it gives you. Also, small machines are rarely much cheaper than standard models, because they are made in fewer numbers and need more or less the same working parts as larger machines. And they are usually fairly basic, lacking many of the refinements offered by larger machines.

However, if you are a one- or two-person household, don't entertain very often and are happy just to have

Below: Appliances these days blend into a kitchen more unobtrusively than ever, owing to the wide availability of décor panels. This kitchen includes a hob, built-under oven, dishwasher, combination washing machine/tumble dryer, cooker hood, fridge and freezer.

Right below: One-piece inset sinks come in many different combinations. This stainless steel one consists of a full-size and a half-size bowl plus a single drainer. The mixer tap is a monobloc type. Right above: The tap shown here is a conventional two-hole mixer. Far right above: This two-hole mixer tap has long handles to allow the hot and cold water to be turned on and off with your elbows when your hands are greasy.

machines that are simply labour-saving, then small equipment will relieve the space problem.

If, on the other hand, your lifestyle and family size demand maximum performance from a tiny kitchen, you'll have to stick with standard equipment but look at how stacking models and machines that do two jobs, such as a washer-dryer or a fridge-freezer, can make the most of the space.

Sinks and taps

Once the poor relation of equipment, the kitchen sink has recently caught the attention of designers as an important area for improvement. And rightly so: it is the centre of the food preparation area and no kitchen could work without it.

Basically the choice is between a sink unit which fits over the base unit, a sink top which is inset in the worktop, or separate bowls and drainers set independently into the worktop.

Although they are the cheapest, sink units that fit over the base unit are losing popularity. They create dirt-collecting joins where they meet the adjacent worktops and the wall behind, and they lack the streamlined sleekness of their drop-in counterparts.

Inset sinks come in various sizes and styles combining sinks, half-sinks and drainers in various permutations from a single sink with drainer upwards.

Separate sinks and drainers give maximum flexibility, as you can buy the number of units you want and arrange them where you like, assuming the appropriate plumbing and water supply are close by. This is an excellent option if you have an awkwardly shaped kitchen and need to site the sink and drainer more than the usual distance apart or on two sides of a corner.

Whichever type you choose, the minimum is a single sink and drainer. If you

have no dishwasher, a double drainer makes washing up easier. Where there's room for it, a second sink—either full- or half-size—is useful for rinsing the detergent from dishes, preparing vegetables or washing hands.

The choice of materials that sinks are made from is on the increase, with synthetics like Corian, Sylac and Resan coming to the fore. These new materials are resistant to rough treatment and most household chemicals, they come in a wide range of colours and, being poor conductors of heat, they stop the water from cooling too rapidly. Even the old favourites have been improved, and now stainless steel is finished with a slightly satin or textured finish to prevent glare and disguise water marks. It is sometimes insulated to reduce noise, too.

Enamelled steel sinks come in a vast range of colours, and some are decorated with a contrasting outline or patterned border. The finish is generally better than it was and will not chip or stain so readily. Ceramic sinks too are much tougher now and come in a good range of colours.

Most new sinks are available with a whole series of optional accessories, all designed to improve efficiency. There are chopping boards to fit over the sink, plate racks to fit inside it, draining baskets, cutlery holders and sink mats to prevent breakages.

The taps to go with the sink can be fitted on it, on the worktop or on the wall behind. Choose pillar (separate) taps or a mixer, which delivers hot and cold water simultaneously from the same swivel spout. Both pillar and mixer taps can be operated by handle or lever; whichever you have should be easy to use even with wet or soapy hands. The newest taps for mixers have a single lever action that controls both temperature and flow.

Mixers are now the most popular but could be a nuisance if you use the kitchen tap for filling the washing machine or for the garden hose; either would leave you with no other water supply.

The range of designs available includes practically everything from 'antique' to space-age, and the finishes are just as varied: chromium plate, enamel, brass, acrylic and any number of new synthetics which, like enamel, come in many different colours.

Before you buy your taps, make sure they are approved by the water authority. It is illegal to install and use (but not to sell) non-approved taps.

Left: The separate drop-in double bowl and drainer in white enamel shown here are a stylish alternative to a one-piece inset sink. They come in a wide range of colours and finishes, and taps are often available to match. Above: A hot-water spray attachment is handy for rinsing dishes or washing hair.

Waste disposers

Getting rid of the more messy kitchen waste like vegetable peelings, food scraps and egg shells is a nuisance, especially if you live in a flat.

An electric waste disposal unit fitted to the sink waste will grind up almost any organic kitchen refuse, reducing it to a pulp which can be washed away through the drainage system. The machine is necessarily noisy—it sounds like an elderly coffee grinder—but as it will be operated for short periods at a time, that shouldn't be a problem. Check that the model you want is approved by the water authority.

Cookers

The main factor governing what cooker you have is the kind of fuel available. If you have ready supplies of gas and electricity you have the greatest choice, but in areas where there is no mains gas, Calor is an alternative.

Gas provides instant, controllable heat while electricity is cleaner to use. Given complete freedom of choice, the current trend is to use a combination of fuels, selecting the most suitable for the job. Broadly, that means gas for the hob and electricity for the oven, though, obviously, individual preferences are the determining factor.

The next decision is whether to buy a free-standing cooker or a built-in hob and oven. Free-standing cookers are cheapest both to buy and to install. They are compact and, as they share most of the refinements of built-ins, you can get a more sophisticated cooking machine for your money. Separate ovens and hobs should really be installed as part of a major kitchen re-vamp, since the work-top has to be cut to take the hob, the oven needs a special housing unit, and fuel supplies may have to be re-routed or extended.

The advantages of built-in cookers are that the separate modules offer you more flexibility when planning the layout, they look smart and they make cleaning easier, as the gaps you get between a free-standing cooker and the neighbouring units are eliminated.

Whether you choose built-in or free-standing, the cooking arrangements are made up in much the same way, consisting of a hob, an oven and a grill.

Hobs

If you choose a gas hob, there will be three or, more often, four burners covered by metal pan supports. The burners may be different sizes for slow, medium or fast cooking, and they are usually surrounded by removable wells to collect spills.

Electric hobs can have radiant rings, hot plates or a glass ceramic surface. All types may incorporate rings, plates or heat areas of different sizes. Radiant rings are coiled elements that glow red when hot. As an energy-saving feature, they sometimes have twin circuit rings, so if you are using a small pan only the centre heats up. Spills collect in a tray beneath the rings to make mopping up easier.

Hot plates are solid black discs sealed into the enamelled hob so spills can't leak down beneath. The plates are sometimes fitted with a thermostatic control to prevent over-heating, a feature which is essential if you do much deep fat frying.

A ceramic hob looks like a sheet of black, brown or white opaque glass, usually with the pan positions marked on it. It is slower to heat up and cool down than radiant rings, though the latest models are more responsive than earlier versions. For safety, choose one that has a warning light, which indicates when the hob is still warm after being switched off. The smooth surface is easy to clean but should be protected from damage by scratching with kitchen knives or grit from vegetables.

Some built-in hobs combine fuels, while others are made up of modular units to incorporate gas burners, electric or ceramic hot-plates, a griddle, deep fat fryer or a barbecue with rotisserie. These separate modules give cooking and kitchen planning the ultimate in versatility.

Ovens

More and more kitchens are adopting the idea of having two ovens, one small and one large, with the smaller containing the grill as well as other heating elements for baking, warming plates, microwave cooking or spit roasting.

In the main oven, either gas or electric, there are at least two shelves and a number of different shelf positions. The door may be solid, or it may have a glass panel or, in the case of electric ovens, an inner glass door, so you can see what progress is being made without letting the heat escape or ruining something which is rising, like a souffle. A light inside is useful for the same reason. For ease of cleaning, choose an oven with a catalytic lining, or an oven that is pyrolytic, which means that fat and splashes can be burnt off in a very hot cycle.

The oven may also double as a grill, if there isn't a separate grill or second oven.

Some electric and gas ovens are fan-assisted, which means warm air is power-circulated to give an even temperature all over the oven. Because of this you can cook at a slightly lower temperature and for a shorter time with the same results, and you can count on food on both the top and bottom shelves cooking at the same rate—a real bonus if you batch-bake for your freezer.

The criticisms most often levelled at fan ovens are that meat roasted in them doesn't taste as good and that food can't be browned quickly at the top of the oven. To overcome this, some ovens are now designed to work with the fan turned on or off as required.

Built-in ovens can be placed at worktop height so you don't have to stoop to take things out. You can also find built-under

Facing page: A built-in oven fits neatly into a run of units and is at a convenient height for taking dishes in and out, and for checking progress through the window in the door. Above: Kitchen equipment is now available in a range of colours like this bright and cheerful electric hob with removable enamel hot plate covers.

Right: The hob shown here features two electric hot plates and two gas rings, to give the best of both worlds. The built-under oven tucks neatly under the hob without interrupting the line of the worktop.

ovens, which are designed to be tucked in under the worktop, saving space; with these, the grill is inside the oven, which means they cannot be used at the same time.

Other options

If you like the looks of a built-in cooker but don't want to go to great expense, there are plenty of free-standing models which, once slotted in to a line-up of units, look like a hob and built-under oven. These new cookers match the dimensions of standard kitchen units and have no eye-level grill to give the game away. Instead, they have a hinged hob lid which, when raised, becomes a neat splashback and, when closed, provides extra work surface.

Cast-iron cookers have a loyal following. Large, warm and cozy, they can be run on solid fuel, wood, oil or gas. Some are designed also to heat your water supply and a limited number of radiators. Because they are kept going all the time, they are particularly suitable for those who do a lot of baking.

Microwave ovens allow food to be cooked in a matter of minutes, or even seconds, with very little added fat or water. The heat is generated not by electric elements or a gas flame, but by the food itself, as its water molecules vibrate rapidly in response to the microwaves. Microwave ovens come in various sizes and may be built-in, wall-mounted or free-standing. A few models are actually incorporated in a conventional gas or electric oven. Most offer a choice of at least two settings, low for defrosting and slow cooking, high for reheating and fast cooking. There are also many optional extras, such as additional settings, a turntable, 'wave stirrers' to ensure even cooking, a browning element, a temperature probe and programming and automatic cooking capabilities.

Left above and below: The cooker hood in the top picture fits into the special housing so that it is invisible when not in use, and only slightly noticeable when pulled out for use. The other type of hood, shown in the picture below (and also on the facing page) fits beneath a short wall unit but is always visible. With both types the fumes and steam from the hob are drawn upwards into the filter before being either re-circulated or expelled outside the house.

Cooker hoods

Clean air is essential to kitchen comfort. A fresh atmosphere and the right level of humidity make for a better living and working environment and will help the decorations last longer, too.

As the cooker, or, more accurately, the hob, is the main source of steam and cooking smells, an electrically operated cooker hood will do most to clear the air.

Cooker hoods should be placed over the hob, between 60 and 90cm above it. They work either by extracting stale air, or by filtering and re-circulating it.

The extractor type is usually fitted to an external wall and vented directly through it. If an outside wall position is not possible—for example, if the hood is suspended over an island unit—then it can be ducted to the nearest external wall. The hood contains a filter to remove grease from the air before expelling it.

Ductless hoods, which draw the air over a charcoal filter to clean it and remove most of the moisture before re-circulating it, can be mounted on any wall, but are generally not as effective as the extractor type. For maximum

Right: A wall-mounted extractor fan is a neat and unobtrusive alternative to a cooker hood. Fitted high on an external wall, it can connect directly into the power supply. Below right and far right: All cooker hoods have a light which illuminates the hob and is a useful supplement to under-shelf tube lighting. Facing page: An alternative to covering appliances with décor panels is to make a positive feature of them. Here the fridge-freezer, dishwasher and washing machine all contribute to the clean, simple lines and modern look.

efficiency, the filter should be replaced regularly.

Many cooker hoods come with both options—extracting and ducting—incorporated in the one unit, so you can choose which to use.

There are two basic shapes of cooker hood: one type is fixed straight on to the wall, leaving room for a wall unit above it; the other fits inside a housing to look like a wall unit. The first type is always visible, but it does give you extra storage if you fit a wall unit above it, while the second is hidden but takes up valuable storage space. Both types have an integral light to illuminate the hob. Some come with two speeds, some with three.

It is not always possible to put a hood above a cooker that has an eye-level grill; in this situation, a powered extractor fan fitted high on an external wall would be the best alternative.

Refrigerators

The size of fridge you need depends on the number of people using it. As a rule of thumb, allow a capacity of about 165–180 litres (which is about 5½–6 cu ft) for a family of four, and add on another 30 litres (1 cu ft) for every extra person in the household. If your requirements are greater than average, for example if you shop infrequently or have to produce three meals a day, every day, you'll need more space.

If you don't have a freezer, you'll need a fridge with an ice box to make ice cubes and store ice cream and small quantities of frozen food. (These are not, however, powerful enough to freeze unfrozen foods.) If you do have a freezer, you would do better to buy a larder fridge; this has no ice box, giving you more space for fridge storage; it's cheaper to run, too.

If you want to incorporate the fridge into a fitted kitchen, you could choose one that will go under the worktop and stand flush with the units next to it. If you want a totally integrated look, choose a model that can be fitted with a décor panel to match the unit doors.

When buying a fridge, check that the storage arrangements—egg holders, bottle racks, salad drawers, shelf positions and so on—suit your needs and that it is easy to clean and de-frost.

De-frosting can be manual, push-button or automatic. Manual needs supervision. You turn off the power, wait for all the ice to melt then pour away the water collected in the drip tray, mop up the rest and turn the power back on again. Push-button is slightly less trouble. You press a button to cut off the power and when the ice is melted, it automatically switches on again. Again, you have to pour away the water. Automatic de-frost never lets the ice build up. The moisture that would have formed

Below right: The fridge-freezer blends into this cottage-style kitchen fairly unobtrusively. With this model the freezer section is quite small relative to the refrigerator and would be useful for storing things that are needed frequently. An additional, larger freezer in the utility room or garage could keep bulk stores needed less often.

into ice is continually channelled out of the cabinet to a reservoir at the back, where it can evaporate into the air.

Freezers

Choose your freezer according to the type and quantity of food you want to store. If you use it to keep food between fairly regular shopping expeditions and for some home-cooked dishes, a medium-sized upright model will be adequate. If you take freezing seriously, bulk-buying frozen food, freezing your own crop of home-grown vegetables or cooking for the freezer in a more systematic and organized way, then a large upright or chest freezer would be more use, but it should be kept somewhere other than the kitchen. As a very rough rule of thumb you should allow approximately 60 litres (2 cu ft) of freezer space per person in the household.

Some manufacturers make upright freezers to match their fridges so they can be stacked, or placed side by side with their doors hinged opposite ways to make a double-doored 'unit'. Inside, the storage space is organized with drawers, flap-fronted shelves or slide-out baskets.

Fridge-freezers

Unless they are kept full, freezers do not work economically. So if you need some capacity for storing frozen food but not enough to merit running a separate freezer, a fridge-freezer would be a good compromise. They come in various sizes, usually with the two sections one on top of the other within the same cabinet but with separate doors. Some very large fridge-freezers have the sections placed side by side with long doors rather like a wardrobe.

The fridge:freezer ratio varies from model to model, and the proportions you choose depend entirely on your own shopping habits and food preferences. Of the vertical ones, some have the fridge at the top and some the freezer. Choose one that has the section you'll use most above, so you don't have to bend down so often.

Fridge-freezers with two compressors offer independent control of both sections and a certain degree of security—if one breaks down, you can shift the food into the section that is still working, until the fault is repaired.

The latest fridge-freezers have a third section, divided from the main part of the refrigerator by a movable vent. Closing the vent raises the temperature in the separate part to the optimum level for storing eggs, cheese, wine and vegetables. This is especially handy if you don't have a separate cool larder.

Décor frames are not so widely available with fridge-freezers but if you think that a large white cabinet would be at odds with the rest of your kitchen, look at the models with coloured cabinets. There isn't an endless spectrum to choose from—usually green, terracotta, bright red and brown—but they do co-ordinate well with the most popular kitchen units.

Dishwashers

Certainly a great labour-saver, a dish-washer saves you time (although it actually takes far longer to do the job); and because the washing is done at high temperatures, it gets things cleaner than by hand.

The machine works most economically when it is loaded right up, so you'll need enough dishwasher-proof crockery to fill it. Most dishwashers have a rinse-and-hold cycle so you can wash away sticky food deposits from the dishes as you put them in throughout the day, and then wash them all together in the evening.

The cheaper the machine, the fewer programmes you can expect, but useful ones to look for are 'economy' (shorter wash at a slightly lower temperature) and 'intensive' for badly soiled dishes. Cheaper machines tend to be much noisier, too, so decide whether quietness is a priority before you buy.

The standard dishwasher capacity is 12 place settings, although some small worktop ones take only three or four while the larger models can hold up to 14. The interior arrangement of racks and baskets varies, so, if you have any especially large or awkwardly shaped plates, dishes or pans that you use regular, check that they will fit in.

Built-in and free-standing models are available. If you are adding the machine to an existing fitted kitchen, make sure it will slide underneath the worktop. If you want total co-ordination, choose one that will take a décor panel.

Laundry equipment

If the kitchen must double as a laundry, aim to have the neatest, most efficient equipment possible and keep it all in the same area.

A plumbed-in front-loading automatic washing machine would be most convenient and least obtrusive in a fitted kitchen.

Top-loading automatics are slimmer and useful in a restricted space, but as they have a lift-up lid, they can't be tucked away under a worktop. One way round this is to site the machine at the end of a run of units and have a hinged section of worktop over it so when the machine is not in use the surface appears to be continuous.

Twin- and single-tub machines are difficult to accommodate neatly and economically even though their siting is not restricted by access to water and drainage—they do not need to be permanently plumbed in and can be wheeled to the sink on wash day. Either could be hidden away behind unit doors, but as their dimensions don't correspond to unit sizes, a good deal of space would be wasted.

Even if you have a garden, you'll probably need some sort of drying equipment for rainy days. Spin dryers extract the maximum of water from clothes, leaving them dry enough to iron or to dry off on a clothes airer. They are

Left: Far from looking clinical, colourful appliances like this dishwasher actually add to the cheeriness of the kitchen. With the range of colours available today, the entire kitchen can be planned to co-ordinate.

comparatively small and mobile and could easily be stored somewhere away from the kitchen, say, in an under-stairs cupboard.

Tumble dryers use warm air to dry clothes, and you can choose to have them bone dry or slightly damp, ready for ironing. The machine disposes of the damp air in one of two ways—it can be either vented to the outside, or condensed and the water drained away. The first type should be placed on an outside wall for direct venting; the condensing type, which is considerably more expensive, does not have to be on an outside wall but does need access to drainage.

To help save space, some manufacturers produce matching, stackable washing machines and tumble dryers. You have to buy a stacking frame to hold them together safely.

If you can, devote a corner of the kitchen to laundry equipment, away from the main work triangle, which should be devoted solely to food preparation. Place a base unit next to the machines to provide storage for washing powder, fabric softener, laundry basket and so on and a surface for putting down the clean clothes when you take them out of the dryer. A slide-out ironing board would make this little laundry area even more self-contained and efficient, and, if the machines take them, décor panels will make it look more streamlined.

Where space won't allow for both a washing machine and a tumble dryer, the best option is a washer/dryer which does both jobs in one piece of equipment. The amount of space it saves is considerable, but the weekly wash will take longer than if you had two separate machines. Also, the machine will not dry the same amount as it washes, so you will have to be on hand to remove part of the load before the drying cycle starts.

Facing page: This large kitchen has plenty of room for appliances like laundry equipment, which is tucked into the peninsular unit at the bottom of the picture. Left: Front-loading washing machines are designed to fit neatly under a worktop and even with the front of the kitchen units.

CHAPTER 6

In the mood

Giving a kitchen a distinctive character may not overcome physical restrictions, but it can disguise or even capitalize on many of the flaws and make the room much nicer to be in.

Left: Bare brick is the perfect choice of material for the walls and newly created arch in this country-style kitchen.

Planning a new look for your kitchen is an exciting prospect, but it is only when you really get down to it that the problems become clear. Often, for example, fitting in all the things you need will make the room look more like a department store at sale time than the stylish kitchen you had set your heart on.

Whether you are limited by space, a small budget, lack of natural light or whatever, a strong positive style will help carry you through.

Ultimately the style you choose will depend on your own individual taste, but remember that the kitchen is just one part of the whole house and, for the sake of continuity, it should relate to the other rooms.

There are fashions in kitchens just as in practically everything else, and trends are reflected in the kinds of units manufacturers make at any given time.

A style doesn't rely just on the units, however. The right blend of colours, textures and patterns along with some carefully selected accessories are just as vital.

Style is an intensely personal thing, but to help you decide which direction to take, we have included in this chapter some suggestions for different ways you might set the scene.

Country house kitchen

This kind of kitchen is the heart of the home, where the family gathers not only to eat but to talk, study or relax. The look is warm and lived-in, the furniture is well used and the atmosphere one of permanence.

The focal point is an important-looking cooker, like a cast-iron one, and the units are of dark-toned wood, probably oak or old pine. The walls give the room colour and maybe texture as well, with bare brick or paint in colours like burnt sienna or ochre. If the plaster is less than perfect, it doesn't matter; as long as it isn't actually crumbling, a few blemishes can only add to the air of maturity.

The floor is of a natural material like flagstones, with Oriental rugs (though not precious ones) to soften the dining area and introduce pattern. The Oriental influence is manifested too in fabrics for curtains and cushions. Paisley, ethnic prints and bold stripes in rich colours will all strike the right note.

A large oak or pine table dominates the room with ladder-backed rush-seated chairs all around. More comfortable furniture in the shape of a couple of armchairs or, if there's room, an old sofa, provides seating for guests who want to chat with the cook while she works. Accessories that reinforce the theme include polished copper and brass, bunches of flowers hung up to dry from the beams, and an assortment of patterned china.

City chic

A family of busy working people needs an efficient kitchen that looks elegant, too. It will be a place where both evening meals and dinner party menus can be produced with a minimum of fuss and then cleared away afterwards leaving the kitchen immaculate.

Perfect planning and plenty of storage are essential to the smooth running of this kitchen. Everything must be built in to make cleaning easy, and there can be no clutter to spoil the sleek lines. The units are laminated, perhaps with a high-gloss polyester finish, in a deep colour like red, bottle green, navy or even black.

For a different but equally elegant effect, plain brilliant white or soft pastel shades are alternatives.

Contrast and pattern, if wanted, can be introduced with floor and wall tiles. Italian-designed ceramics come in some very stylish abstract patterns that would complement this setting very well. At the window, a crisp, plain-coloured roller blind or, perhaps, a venetian blind would be appropriate.

If all the sparseness makes the room uncomfortably bleak, add a few decorative touches in the shape of an ultra-modern pendant light hung low over the breakfast bar; a couple of sculptural, tubular steel stools and a pot-planted tree —a spiky yucca or a lemon tree are both suitably exotic.

Bright and cheery

Younger and more relaxed than city chic but still right for the working family, a streamlined kitchen all in white with splashes of bright primaries makes a cheerful place to cook.

Again surfaces are extra-practical with laminates playing a major role, but here the severity is countered with coloured edges or wooden handles and trims. On the floor, vinyl sheet in a plain tile or grid pattern looks smart, and for the walls a co-ordinating splashback of geometric-patterned ceramic tiles or plain ones with contrasting grouting.

On show are pots and pans in brilliant enamel along with sets of utensils with coloured handles, hung from equally vivid grid wall racks. Both add impact to the two-colour scheme.

Facing page: Features of a country-style kitchen include a stripped pine or oak table and chairs, a cast-iron cooker, natural flooring such as quarry tiles, exposed beams, and either a dresser, open shelving or natural wood units.
Left and above: These two examples of 'city chic' show the sleek, streamlined elegance that is a feature of this type of kitchen.

Above left: The emphasis is on functionalism in the hi-tech food laboratory kitchen. Efficient catering is the objective, and equipment is large and robust. All surfaces are totally practical, and ornaments are kept to a bare minimum. Above right: Totally opposite in feeling is the ecology kitchen, which is characterized by natural materials like wood and brickwork. Traditional cooking utensils, baskets and glass storage jars filled with whole foods are all much in evidence on open shelves. Facing page: The modern version of a Victorian kitchen utilizes stripped pine or painted wood furniture for storage, with plenty of old-fashioned crockery or ornaments on display. It's important that the sink, taps, appliances, wall covering and tiles do not look too modern.

In a kitchen designed for people on the move, a slim car radio could be fixed to the underside of a wall unit. A wall-mounted telephone is indispensable and, if the kitchen is in a large family house, an intercom is useful for calling the hungry to table!

Food laboratory

A no-frills kitchen designed exclusively for cooking appeals to those with a taste for hi-tech. The look is austere but, in practice, the kitchen is extremely functional, using ideas and even equipment from restaurant kitchens.

Glass, stainless steel, zinc, marble and tile are the predominant materials—all hard, cold but immensely serviceable.

The cooker is large, robust and, like most of the other appliances, probably bought from a caterer's supplier. Storage is provided by open shelves made from metal grille. They're loaded with capable-looking aluminium pans, white mixing bowls and ingredients kept in matching glass jars arranged in serried ranks.

The walls, if not completely tiled, are painted white, the floor is laid with linoleum or studded rubber to deaden the noise and, at the window, white or metallic fine-slatted venetian blinds cut out the glare on sunny days.

Ecology kitchen

This low-tech kitchen is the complete opposite of the Food Laboratory, and those who yearn for the good life will feel at home in it. Materials are natural and the style simple. Units are made from pale new wood, and décor panels fitted to the essential machines hide the unacceptable face of technology. For the floor, stripped boards are an obvious choice, and for the worktops, end-grain hardwood. Quarry tiles or slate are alternative surfaces for both.

The walls are painted plain matt white with more quarries or timber cladding for the splashback. For an even more rustic flavour, the walls could be stripped back to brick and then painted to accentuate the texture. At the windows, Roman blinds made from unbleached calico or batik fabric fall into gentle folds. And on the window sill below stands a large, deep container—an old fireclay sink, an enormous stew pot or a pottery foot bath—in which a herb garden grows for most of the year.

Storage is a mixture of cupboards and open shelves. The shelves are ranged with glass-stoppered jars filled with dried fruit, pulses, pasta and spices, which bring colour, and shallow willow baskets piled with neatly folded linen tea-towels.

The equipment is traditional; copper bowls, terracotta casseroles, Kilner jars, wooden spoons and birch-twig whisks all add to the wholesome earthiness.

Victorian villa

If you've furnished the rest of your house with old and antique furniture, a purely functional kitchen will seem out of context—and the chances are you won't enjoy it much, either. A better way would be to bring some nostalgia into the kitchen and temper it with a little functionalism to get the right balance of decorative effect and practicality.

Start by incorporating some antique furniture into the planned layout. What you include depends mainly on your resources and the size of the room, but a large scrubbed pine table and a dresser are essential ingredients. Other possible candidates are a chest of drawers, a chiffonier, a sideboard and antique school- and shop-fittings.

In fact, kitchens in Victorian days

relied upon the dresser and the walk-in larder for storage, more than on built-in cupboards. But you may feel that you cannot do without units, despite the Victorian theme.

If you do opt for units, the style is crucial to the look. Go for either natural wood in a mellow finish, or painted wood, and choose a design with plenty of character and detail. Look for cupboard doors with fielded panels and leaded lights, coving at the top or fretwork pelmets below and built-in display shelves with galleried edges.

Try to avoid glaring white equipment, choosing instead cream or brown, or buy models that will take décor panels. Sinks too are better off-white—or you might even come across a fireclay butler's sink with wooden draining boards, which would be perfect. Hardwood is best for the worktop, with a marble slab set into it if you make a lot of pastry. If the cost of the wood is prohibitive, opt for tiles or laminate in a rich colour that will blend well. If you can find them, decorative original Victorian tiles, salvaged from old fireplaces or washstands, make a beautiful splashback. Try to avoid taps that are too modern in feeling. Plain, simple pillar taps or a traditional-style mixer would look much more appropriate.

For the floor, stripped boards, parquet or cork are all good. For the walls, choose between paint in dusky shades of cream, pink, duck-egg blue or pale green, or wallpaper in an exuberant floral pattern. The windows could be dressed with café curtains hung from a brass or dark wood pole or with wooden-slatted venetian blinds.

The nostalgia buff is by nature a magpie and can use the kitchen as yet another showcase for his or her finds. Collections of china and pottery jugs and plates, framed pictures and all kinds of kitchenalia could be displayed here.

CHAPTER 7

Room for improvement

With a little ingenuity, overcoming difficulties like lack of space, having to eat in the kitchen, poor light and shortage of funds is not impossible.

Here are some ideas to get you thinking along the right lines. Put them to work to improve your kitchen, or follow the general guidelines and adapt them to your own needs.

Space stretching

Any kitchen is easier to plan if it is a regular shape with no awkward corners, nooks or crannies; but if it is small as well as irregular, you have a double problem.

Begin by removing the obstacles. Re-route or box in pipework. Re-site windows and doors if they seriously upset your plans. Demolish built-in larders if they stand in the way of a better storage scheme. Block off unnecessary doorways. Re-hang interior doors so that they swing out of the room, or remove them altogether.

Valuable extra space can be gained by building an extension, but this is an expensive solution and one that might involve you in planning permission difficulties. Alternatively, extend into the house by taking down all or part of the wall between the kitchen and dining room, or annex some of the hall so you can use the valuable space under the stairs. Another possibility would be to swap rooms—exchange the dining room for the kitchen so you have a spacious area for cooking and a cozy, intimate dining recess.

If you have no choice but to put up with a tiny kitchen, try to make the best of it. Hunt around for equipment that is less than standard depth so you can make the worktops and cupboards shallower from front to back. After all, in most kitchens, the part of the worktop nearest the wall is used more for storage than for working. Use the corners fully by slotting in a cooker diagonally across a corner or putting a separate sink and drainer in an L-shaped arrangement around it.

Use the walls to their full capacity. System shelving can provide a whole bank of adjustable storage and, if you're worried about dust and dirt, you could fit floor-to-ceiling concertina or bi-fold doors to cover them completely. Make maximum use of the shelves by buying stacking china and pans, and cutlery that hangs from its own rack. Screw hooks into the undersides of shelves to hang utensils, cups and gadgets.

High-level shelves can be fixed to run all round the room or across it to provide more storage for the things you use less often. A pulley—the kind usually used for airing clothes—together with some butchers' hooks can make a wonderful overhead rack from which to hang pots, pans, colanders, baskets and so on. Similarly, a slim curtain pole or some dowelling fixed along the wall between the worktop and wall units can be hung with all kinds of smaller gadgets.

To make the room appear larger than it is, there are a number of visual tricks you can try. First, cut out clutter—it makes any room seem cramped and over

Below: A lot can be made of a cramped space with careful planning. Here, two double-burner hobs have been installed in separate shallow worktops, and an oven is placed diagonally to use a corner fully. Built-in shelving adds valuable storage area without taking up extra space.

Right: One way to fit a table at which to have meals into a small kitchen is to position it in the centre of the room. It will also serve as an extra work surface for preparing food. This table is topped with tiles, to blend with the décor and provide a durable, easy-to-clean finish.

crowded. Keep pattern to the minimum; it is much better to stick to large areas of one or two colours. By extending the floor covering up on to the unit plinths, the floor area appears larger; and by using the same colour and material for the worktop and splashback you can make the surfaces seem wider.

Eating in the kitchen

If the kitchen is the main eating area, make it as attractive as a separate dining room would be.

You won't be able to hide the kitchen completely so make sure it looks good and complements the style of the dining area. The dining furniture must be tough enough to stand up to kitchen life but still smart or your guests will feel they're being entertained 'below stairs'. Arrange the furniture prettily, in front of French windows with a view of the garden or in an alcove—create it as an entity, slightly separate from the business end of the room.

A cooker hood, or at least an extractor fan, is also important, so you won't have to eat in an atmosphere of steam and cooking odours.

You can play down the working rôle of the room by having different floor levels for the two parts—the dining area should be lower than the kitchen and preferably separated by a partition of units, with a raised serving shelf along the back so diners don't have a clear view of the debris.

A dishwasher would be a great asset in this kind of kitchen, as the cook must learn to be tidy and dirty dishes could be loaded straight into the machine rather than standing round in unappetizing piles.

Clever lighting can also contribute to a kitchen/dining room. Choose tungsten instead of fluorescent, as its warm glow is softer and more welcoming. Also, have the kitchen and dining area lights separately switched so that when you all sit down to eat, the kitchen lights can be turned off, rendering the work-area invisible.

Letting in the light

A gloomy kitchen is a depressing place indeed, but there are ways to increase the daylight or maximize what you've got.

It is certainly worth spending money to get more daylight. If your kitchen is undergoing major changes, take the opportunity to increase the number or size of the windows. Or, if the kitchen is in a single-storey extension or has a roof of its own, install a roof light.

Roof lights give bright, overall light even on cloudy days, but they should be double glazed to reduce heat loss. Unless the kitchen faces south, blinds fitted to the roof lights may not be used very often, but you will appreciate them on sunny days when the kitchen gets too hot for comfort.

If you prefer to take less drastic action, replace the exterior and interior doors with glass ones and paint the window reveals white to reflect more incoming light.

Decorate to maximize the available daylight by using pale colours for the walls, floors and ceilings and shiny reflective surfaces for the units, worktops and splashbacks. A mirrored splashback will pick up a lot of light but it will only look good when perfectly clean; also, it will visually double worktop clutter, so it may not be such a good idea.

Use artificial light cleverly. Illuminate open shelves with spotlights or concealed under-shelf strips. Cupboards in dark corners should be lit from inside. If your kitchen is incurably dungeon-like, you might consider installing an illuminated ceiling.

Beating the budget

Provided you spend time on planning, creating an efficient kitchen on a limited budget is not too difficult.

If you're starting from scratch, shop around for units and equipment, as prices vary from shop to shop. Visit the sales and discount warehouses for goods at dramatically reduced prices, remembering that as long as equipment is in working order, flaws in the paintwork can be dealt with easily. The For Sale columns in local papers are another good source of kitchen bargains.

Whether you buy second-hand or want to improve the existing kitchen fittings, you can achieve a great deal for very little cost. Mismatched units can be made to look uniform if you paint them all the same colour. Just wash them thoroughly, rub down with fine glasspaper and then paint with oil-based gloss or eggshell paint. A set of matching replacement handles and a continuous worktop to span the newly co-ordinated line-up will complete the transformation.

A couple of coats of paint can also transform old units that you are tired of. Even just replacing the handles can perk them up considerably.

If you want to colour-match the equipment, that too can be painted,

Left: If the design of the house allows, a roof light is an excellent way to light up a gloomy kitchen. Above: If you have a dark cupboard which is hard to see into, fitting interior strip lights with door-operated switches is the ideal solution. Two strips lights have been used here, concealed behind false valances to protect them and act as light baffles.

Right above and inset: If your kitchen units are in the right position but just look old-fashioned, you can give them a face-lift by simply replacing the doors, drawer fronts and, if desired, the worktop. Whether your existing doors are the lay-on type (which means they hide the framework or carcass) or the older type that hang within the framework, you should replace them with lay-on doors. Right below: An even less expensive way to brighten up your kitchen units is to fix a self-stick wallpaper border on to the doors and drawer fronts, edged with decorative moulding. Running the same border above a tiled splashback gives a co-ordinated effect.

except for the cooker and central heating boiler, which get too hot. For best results, use car spray paint and do the job carefully, using masking tape and polythene sheets to protect the insides of the machines, the door seals and any trims you don't want to colour. Car paint comes in a good range of colours, including some metallic ones which look very stylish when used for kitchen units.

If your fitted kitchen is in good condition but you don't like the way it looks, replacement doors will give it a major

facelift at a fraction of the cost of a new kitchen. There are a number of manufacturers who will make to measure unit door and drawer fronts in wood or laminate finishes and deliver them ready to be screwed on.

Alternatively, you could re-face existing doors and drawers with one of the attractive new laminates. A laminated worktop can also be re-faced, or you could replace it with a new hardwood or tiled one.

If you are starting with nothing and your resources are at rock bottom, spend what you have on essential equipment and build up from there, as and when you can. To begin with, a perfectly adequate kitchen can be made from a worktop with open shelves above and below, all supported on wall brackets. Later on, you can replace the low-level shelves with base units, and later still, the high-level ones with wall units.

As long as you stick to a permanent basic layout and you won't want to change the positions of plumbing, power and lighting in the future, building a kitchen piece by piece can work very well, as it gives you time to work out your priorities. The only snag is that the units you choose may be discontinued before your kitchen is complete. If this happens, and you can't get wall cupboards from the same range as the base units, look around for a style that complements the originals rather than opting for a close, but not close enough, match.

When there's nothing wrong with a kitchen except that it looks jaded, a set of new, colour-matched accessories, pans, tea towels, serving dishes and storage jars can do a great deal to pep it up. Add new tiles (you can fix them over the old ones), or just tile grouting 'paint' to cover grubby grouting. Change the wall colour and re-think the window treatment, and it will look a completely different room.

Decorative touches make a contribution out of all proportion to their cost. Posters and prints—especially if food is the subject matter—or framed collections of labels from wine, citrus fruits or canned foods can make a plain wall into an important focal point.

Left: A system based on low-cost bricks, chipboard and inexpensive softwood gives you a fitted kitchen at a fraction of the price of ready-made units. It's easy to build and very versatile, as you can build new units to fit around your existing appliances, add new features like a breakfast bar, or replan the kitchen from scratch. And it also gives you the facility of starting out fairly simply, with open base units, then when your budget allows, you can add matching doors. Above: Décor and accessories go a long way towards brightening up a kitchen, and re-thinking this aspect may be all that's needed to give yours a new lease of life.

CHAPTER 8

Behind closed doors

Bathrooms these days are warmer and cozier, as well as more practical and functional than ever before. The basics are still the same—but the overall effect is much improved.

The bathroom is a paradoxical room: it is the most private place in the house and yet surprisingly public—guests are more likely to see it than they are the kitchen. It must be practical but at the same time warm and comfortable: weekday ablutions can't take more than a few minutes, yet when you've time to spare, there's nothing so relaxing as a long, luxurious, scented bath. It has to be designed for efficiency, plus easy cleaning and maintenance, but it must, above all, be a haven—a place that is pleasant and cheerful in the morning when you're preparing to face the world, and restful at night when you're getting ready for bed.

Until recently, bathrooms were very much an afterthought in terms of interior design. Because of the expense and upheaval of re-plumbing, any major improvements were avoided as, hour for hour, the amount of time the family spent in the room didn't justify the cost. In short, the bathroom was a low priority area.

Now all that is changing. For most people, bathing is more than a once-a-week affair; and bathrooms, like kitchens, are expected to reflect the increased use by being attractive as well as functional. They must suit the lifestyle of everyone using them, and sometimes even perform a dual role.

If your bathroom falls short of the ideal, there are a number of ways you can improve it. But you must be prepared to devote careful thought to the planning and, depending on what's to be done, set aside a realistic budget.

Extent of the problem

Before you call the plumber or buy the tiles, decide exactly what you want and how much work is needed to effect the transformation. Begin by appraising the bathroom as it stands, and consider which of the following categories it falls into. Is it cold, dark, antiquated and prone to condensation, with visible pipework and audible plumbing? Or is it perhaps dated, dingy and not particularly convenient, with few creature comforts? Or is it just dull—modern, perfectly serviceable but rather bleak and lack-lustre? By assessing the existing faults you'll get a clearer view of which improvements are essential and which desirable.

If your bathroom falls into the 'antiquated' category, a complete re-fit is probably the best course of action. You can expect total refurbishment to cost anywhere from a few hundred to a few thousand pounds, but it will be a valuable longterm investment. Apart from the pleasure and satisfaction it gives you, when the time comes to sell your house, a beautiful bathroom is as much of a marketable feature as a modern fitted kitchen.

If you live in a rented house or flat and your landlord shows no signs of updating the bathroom, there are plenty of ways you can inject new life without going to great expense.

Bathrooms in the 'inconvenient' category can be made more practical and comfortable by adding extra facilities and perhaps changing the layout. Clever decorating ideas using soft textures and warm colours will do a lot to make it more pleasant to be in.

It may seem extravagant to spend time, effort and money on bathrooms in the third category, which are perfectly adequate but just dull. After all, if they're properly equipped with modern fittings, what's the problem? Well, if for just a little money you can exchange an uninspiring, characterless room for one that's colourful, stylish and full of personality, why not do it?

Whatever the extent of the improvements, your answers to the questions which follow will help pinpoint exactly what you want.

Crucial questions

Are you adding a new bathroom where none existed before, or are you re-fitting an old one?

If you are re-fitting your old bathroom, any plumbing work will probably be fairly straightforward as long as you stick to the same layout. As soon as you start actually re-positioning or adding extra equipment, costs begin to rise and the work has to comply with local building regulations.

Converting a spare room, a section of a large bedroom or any other under-used space into a second bathroom is an excellent idea and one that will add to the value of your home. The new bathroom should be sited within easy reach of existing drainage and, again, the plans must comply with local building regulations. Ideally, you should try to use existing soil pipes and stacks if this is possible, as installing new ones is an expensive business.

Extending hot and cold water supplies is more straightforward, but it is still bound to mean some disruption. In some circumstances it may be better simply to extend the rising main and then install an instantaneous electric or gas water heater to supply the basin, shower or bathtub.

Will it be en-suite with the master bedroom or completely separate?

An en-suite bathroom is a real luxury and a great asset as far as property value is concerned, but don't lose sight of the mundane practicalities. If you want coloured sanitaryware, choose it bearing in mind that the bedroom and bathroom should be decorated to co-ordinate with each other, and therefore, as the bathroom fittings are perhaps the most permanent fixtures, the colour scheme for

Below left: Fitting a basin in a bedroom will help to relieve the pressure on the bathroom. A vanity unit looks especially nice in these surroundings. Below right: If extending existing water supplies to the bedroom is not practical, it may be simpler to install an instantaneous shower, which takes cold water from the rising main and heats it to the required temperature.

both rooms will be influenced by them for years to come.

In a small house, it may be very tempting to make a bathroom adjoining the main bedroom en-suite just by blocking off the original door and making a communicating one. However, if the bathroom contains the only wc in the house, there *must* be access other than through the bedroom.

Who will use the bathroom? Will it be exclusively yours or will the whole family share it?

In a family house, an en-suite bathroom does help to alleviate the morning rush but if one bathroom has to be shared by the whole household, there are still ways to relieve the pressure.

You can double up on washing facilities within the bathroom by installing twin basins and having a shower cubicle as well as the bath. Keeping the wc separate from the main bathroom will also make life easier. If it isn't already separate, it shouldn't be too difficult to make it so by building a partition wall with a door connecting it with the bathroom or, better still, with an adjacent hallway.

Fitting everyone's possessions into a relatively small space is the other problem. Plenty of cupboard and shelf space will take care of most of the clutter, but things in constant use, that have to be left out, should be arranged neatly, too. In households of three or more, individual tooth mugs, towel rails, dressing gown pegs and hooks for sponge bags arranged in groups will help keep things in order, as will colour-coded toothbrushes, face cloths and towels.

In a heavily used bathroom at least one towel rail that is either heated or hung over a radiator is essential, to prevent damp towels from forming a soggy mountain as the rush hour rolls on. The type with two bars is especially useful.

Does the bathroom contain the only washing and lavatory facilities in the house?

If so, it is well worth thinking about putting additional washing and lavatory facilities elsewhere. For example, a vanitory basin or shower could be fitted into a bedroom. 'Dead' space on the landing could be converted into a shower room. The space under the stairs, fitted with a wc and tiny hand basin, could become a useful downstairs cloakroom. Don't worry if none of these odd spaces has a window—an extractor fan is a per-

fectly efficient and legal meals of ventilation.

If you are installing a shower cubicle in a bedroom without creating a separate bathroom, you must make sure there are no plug points within 2.5m of the shower.

A second bathroom or a cloakroom being installed off the kitchen has to have a lobby, containing either a window or an extractor fan, between the wc and the kitchen.

Does the family include any small children or elderly folk? If not, is there any possibility that it will do in the future?

When the family includes young children or old people, the bathroom should be designed with them in mind. Safety is always important, but children and the elderly are more vulnerable than most, so special precautions should be taken.

Make sure shower trays and baths are non-slip. If they don't have an integral non-slip surface, use adhesive strips or rubber mats which stick to the base with suction pads. Neither of these is very attractive but they do the job. A grab-rail next to the bath will make getting in and out easier.

Never leave puddles of water on a smooth floor: they make it slippery. And while cushioned vinyl might not be such a hard surface to fall on, in a bathroom there are plenty of metal and ceramic fittings that could do real damage to anyone falling against them.

Scalding is a considerable danger, especially if there is a shower, so only fit the kind that is thermostatically controlled to keep water at a constant, preselected temperature and to cut out if it rises higher.

As both generations are sensitive to cold, the bathroom should be well heated, but don't position any radiator or heater where it could accidentally come into contact with bare skin. Much better to site a heater high on the wall, or to protect a radiator by boxing it into a grille-fronted cabinet.

The bath, too, could be boxed in, giving it a wide surround that would provide a place to sit while drying and dressing.

A lockable medicine cabinet is a must when children are around. But elderly people will use it too, so choose one with a locking device that will fox the little ones without being too fiddly for arthritic fingers. The door lock is also important. Fit one which can be opened from the

Below left: Unused space under the stairs can sometimes be converted into a handy cloakroom. Below right: Even the relatively simple procedure of fitting a second basin in a bathroom will help to alleviate the morning rush.

Right: If you are lucky enough to have a really large bathroom, you can also make it into a dressing room, a laundry room or, like the room shown here, simply an oasis of luxury.

outside in case a child gets stuck or an older person takes ill or has a fall.

How much space is there? Could the room be put to another use when it is not fulfilling its intended role?

In a large bathroom it may seem a great waste to use the space only twice a day, but there are other ways it can earn its living. Easy-clean surfaces and a handy water supply make it the perfect place to put on make-up, style hair and do a manicure or pedicure. Fitness enthusiasts who take the body-beautiful even more seriously might want to kit it out with an exercise cycle, rowing machine, yoga mats, weights and wall bars, together with a hospital-style weighing machine to keep an accurate check on progress.

For those who enjoy a little luxury, a bathroom-cum-dressing room provides an oasis of peace in which to get ready for the day. Banks of full-length mirrors to reflect front and back views, a large wardrobe, a comfortable chair and, if there's room, a chest of drawers or dressing table will complete the metamorphosis. An extractor fan would be a good idea, however, to disperse steam quickly.

On a more practical level, the bathroom can double as a laundry. With ready access to water and drainage, it is the ideal location. For safety's sake, the washing machine and tumble dryer must not be within reach of anyone using the bath or shower, and the equipment must be permanently plumbed in and wired to a switched socket *outside* the room by a qualified electrician.

Laundry equipment does nothing for the aesthetics of the bathroom, so conceal it if you can. In a spacious room, by losing 60cm off one side, you could convert a wall into a kind of laundry cupboard by lining up the machines together with kitchen units and a worktop to keep

Left: In a fairly spacious bathroom, a raised area near the bath, carpeted and furnished with pillows, atmospheric lighting and tropical plants, creates a dramatic, opulent effect.

all the soap powders and washing aids. Bi-fold doors fitted at either side would close off the whole area when it's not being used.

If this arrangement is too space consuming, the two machines could be stacked in a tall cupboard, like an airing cupboard, to take up the minimum of floor area.

On the face of it, making the bathroom serve a double purpose is a sensible idea, but do consider the implications. If the bathroom in question is the only one, do you really want a teenage daughter to practise different styles of make-up, or the family yoga expert her lotus position while the rest of you queue patiently outside?

Making it happen

While it is possible to buy bathroom fittings quite cheaply, installing them can be expensive. Plumbing is simpler now than ever before, and some jobs can be tackled successfully by a diy expert. However, linking up new fittings with old supply pipes might prove too much for even the most tenacious amateur, so know your limitations. An out-of-commission bathroom is even more disruptive than a non-functioning kitchen so, for the sake of domestic harmony, it may be better to spend a bit more to have the job done quickly by professionals.

You can, of course, save money by getting your builder to do the jobs that affect the essential working of the bathroom, leaving you to cope with the cosmetics like decorating, tiling and carpentry.

If you want to opt out of all but the planning, design and decision making, you'll need a fair amount of funds. If this poses a problem, there are a couple of ways you can try to raise the cash.

First, banks and building societies are usually happy to lend money for home improvements and, if you are a home owner and the work is being done in your main residence, you should qualify for tax relief on the interest.

Second, if the improvements are urgently needed because your bathroom is archaic or non-existent, approach your local environmental health officer to find out if there is any possibility that you will be eligible for a grant.

CHAPTER 9

Winning the space race

The more time and thought that go into the planning and design of a bathroom, the more convenient, comfortable and attractive it will be.

The simplest way to re-vamp a bathroom is to replace the old fittings with modern ones of the same size. This keeps plumbing and decorating costs down yet gives the room a fresh new look. However, if the trouble with the original bathroom is that it is cramped and inconvenient as well as shabby, then the new one should be designed to overcome those problems with a better layout.

Help and advice

Because plumbing, building regulations and space all impose restrictions, devising the perfect layout is quite tricky. Help and advice can be obtained from a number of sources.

An architect or bathroom specialist will be able to turn your dreams into reality with comparatively little effort but a fair amount of expense on your part. If you want to use professional design skills but are prepared to employ the various workmen and supervise the job yourself, you may be interested in one of the mail order planning services offered by some sanitaryware manufacturers to anyone intending to use their products. Some of these services are free; others make a nominal charge.

If you are happy to draw up the plans, then a good builder and plumber between them will make the necessary structural changes, sort out the pipework, fit the equipment and decorate the room, overcoming any problems you may not have thought of.

The local builders' merchant is a good place to seek general advice, especially if you are looking for a special product to help overcome a particular design snag, such as a small bath or wall-mounted taps.

To make sure you don't commit any serious errors, contact the local authority and water board who will give you a disheartening list of things you can and can't (mostly can't) do.

No architect, designer or builder can create your ideal bathroom unless he is properly briefed. It is a bit like going to the hairdresser's—unless you have very firm opinions about what you want, it is easy to give the professional a free hand to experiment with ideas he has been longing to try or, perhaps worse, to give you a similar bathroom to the one that has satisfied his last half-dozen clients. Unfortunately, unlike a disastrous hair style which will grow out in a matter of weeks, a bathroom is a fixture you have to live with for years.

Making plans

To be sure the bathroom is designed to suit you, work out your own plan *before* you consult the professionals. Consider all the possibilities including the ones that don't look immediately viable, and involve the rest of the family so they can have a say, too. Put your ideas on paper —not just a vague list of thoughts but a properly drawn out plan. This done, when you call in the architect or builder,

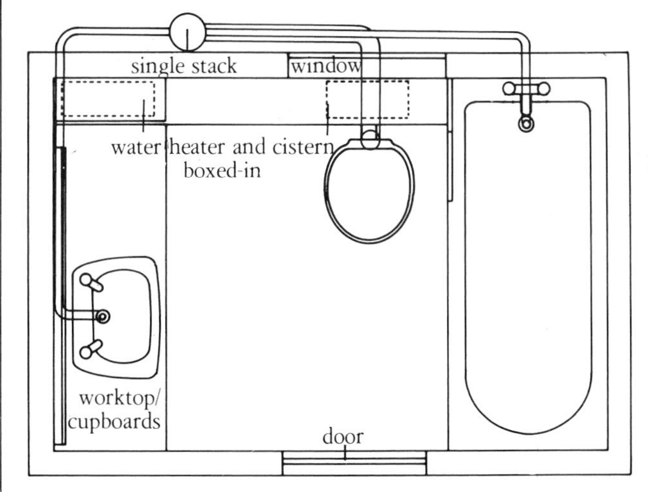

Above: This bathroom offers plenty of scope for conversion. Left and below: The floor plan and sketch show one possible way to convert it. The basin has been moved to a better position and boxed in to add storage space. The cistern has been boxed in as well, but it has not been moved. The water heater is also enclosed.

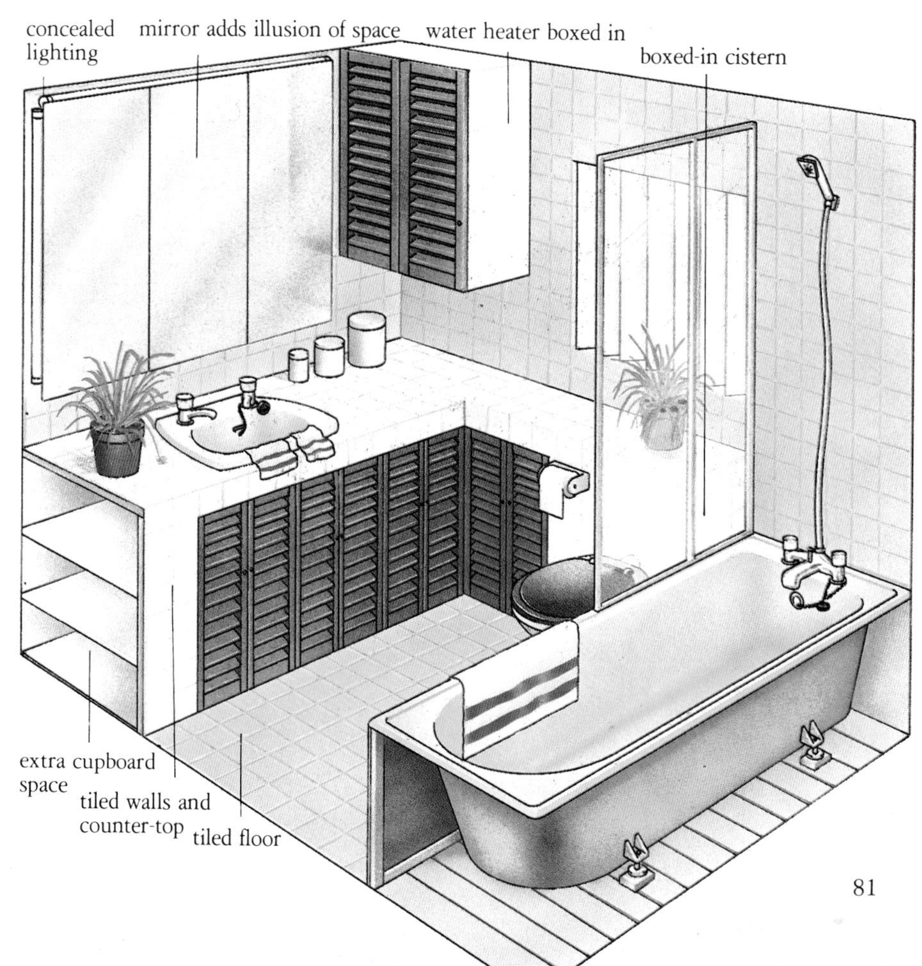

Right and far right: This efficient but rather dingy bathroom has been transformed simply by replacing the suite and redecorating, incorporating new tiles and flooring.

there'll be more chance of a mutual understanding, allowing you to use their experience and expertise productively to make things happen that you thought were impossible.

Bathroom planning is very similar to kitchen planning but with even more constraints. Begin by gathering together a collection of catalogues so you can mull over the range of fittings available, then make a list of the ones you would like to include. At this stage, list your maximum requirements—you can trim it down later if necessary.

Next, draw rough plans of the bathroom floor area and walls, marking in the doors, windows, radiators, built-in cupboards and so on, and indicating the positions of waste pipes and water supply. Label your roughs with all the appropriate measurements, checking them twice before you write them down. (Builders' materials are now sold in metric sizes, so, to avoid confusion, measure the room in metric, using an expanding steel rule rather than a tape measure.)

Picturing your bathroom

Now, you can make an accurate scale plan. For this you'll need graph paper, a sharp pencil, a ruler, eraser, some thin card and coloured pencils or felt-tip pens.

Draw the floor plan, marking the positions of waste pipes, doors and cupboards, including their opening arcs. Now draw four elevations to the same scale, one for each wall, again showing the exact positions of windows, doors, pipework and any other fixture or obstruction.

Positioning the fittings is the next task. It is not simply a matter of squeezing everything in but of arranging the elements logically, making the most economical use of the existing plumbing

arrangements and allowing enough space for them to be used comfortably.

Dimensions and user space

Work out the measurements of the fittings you will be using. If you are keeping existing sanitaryware, you can measure that; but if you are buying new pieces, the brochures should give you exact dimensions. The measurements given here should only be used as a rough guide.

The standard British bath is about 1,700mm long and 700mm wide, though you can get shorter, longer, narrower and wider versions. Baths are usually about 500mm high, though you can get them with lower sides. Shower trays are normally between about 600 and 900mm square.

Basins vary in size, but two standard sizes are 635mm wide by 455mm deep, and 560mm wide by 405mm deep. The rim, for adults, should be about 815mm from the floor.

The size of a wc can vary too, but you can allow roughly 500mm in width and 700 to 800mm in depth (from the wall to the rim). The height to the top of the cistern will be about 800mm. Bidets are around 400mm wide and 600mm deep (from wall to rim).

In addition, you need to allow 'user spaces' adjacent to each piece of sanitaryware. These measurements are: for a wc or bidet, an area 800mm wide and 600mm deep; for a basin, 1,000mm wide and 700mm deep; for a shower enclosed on three sides, 750mm wide and 700mm deep (a shower enclosed on only one or two sides needs the same width but a user space depth of only 400mm); and for a bath, a rectangle 1,100mm by 700mm, with the long side running along the length of the bath, preferably from the taps' end.

Allow headroom of at least 2,200mm

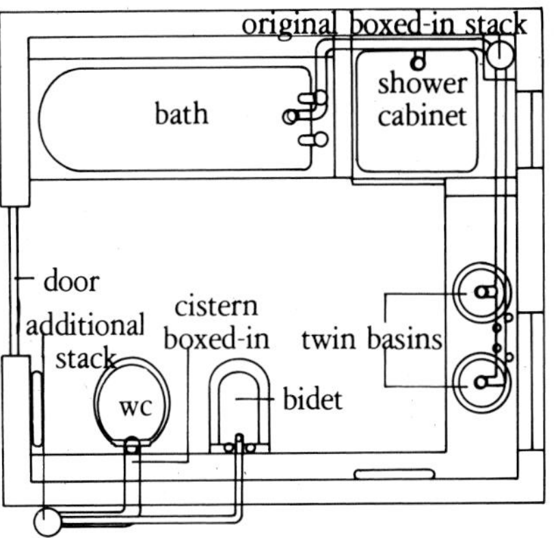

Far left: In this old house, the separate bathroom and wc are both cramped, the fittings awkwardly placed and the plumbing and wiring obsolete. Left: One possible conversion, shown in this floor plan, makes the wc and bathroom into one. The positions of the bath and wc are interchanged, and a new soil stack installed inside the house. Below: A sketch of the conversion shows how the new room accommodates a bidet and shower. Mirrors above the boxed-in wc cistern add to the feeling of space.

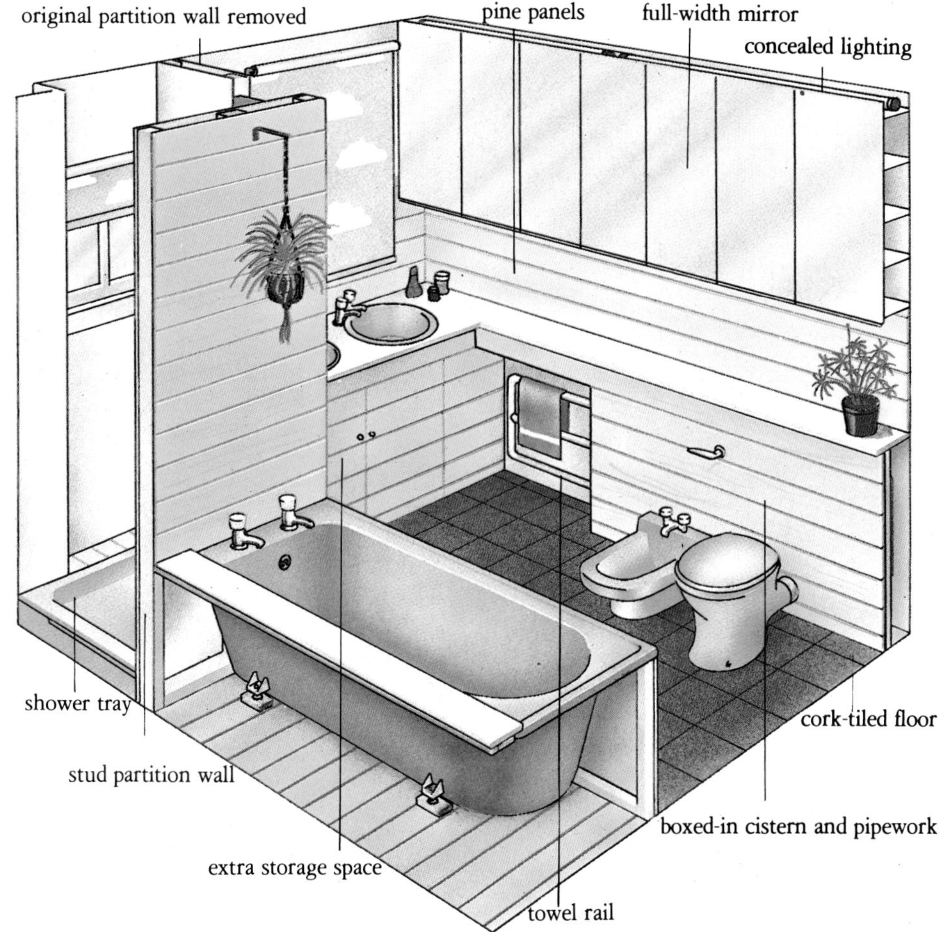

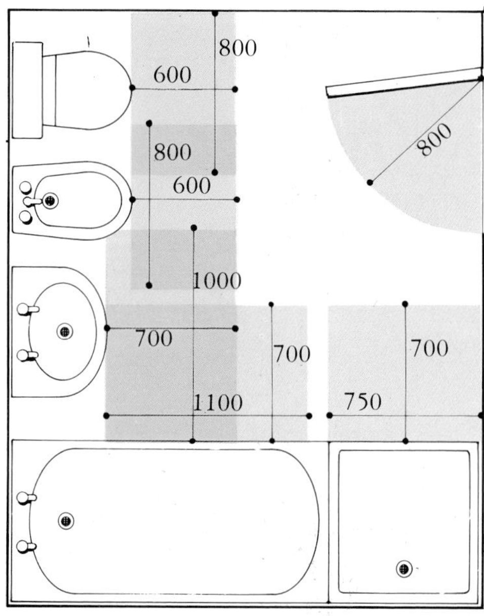

Above: When designing a bathroom, make sure that you include sufficient room for actually using the fittings (and to allow for opening the door). Recommended user spaces for each item are shown here. Note that the user spaces can overlap where necessary. Right: A heated towel rail is an effective way to keep towels dry and tidy. Facing page: Controllable ventilation is essential in a bathroom, and an extractor fan fitted at the source of the steam is one way of controlling condensation.

at the bath, shower and basin where the user will be standing; you can get away with 2,000mm for the bidet and wc, which is useful if you want to tuck them below a sloping ceiling or the stairs.

If you're placing a wc, bidet or basin adjacent to a wall, shower cubicle or airing cupboard, make sure there's enough clearance for elbows and knees—anything less than 250mm would be a tight squeeze.

Using the same scale as for the room plan, cut out shapes from thin card to represent all the fittings you hope to include, and rectangles to represent their user spaces. To make the juggling easier, pair the fittings and their respective rectangles by marking them with colour. Now arrange them on your floor plan, constantly checking the elevation for vertical obstructions.

Important factors

As the wc is the most difficult and expensive thing to move, it is a good idea to begin by placing it in its original spot. If by moving it, however, you would make the bathroom more convenient, or if you are installing a wc in a bathroom which didn't previously have one, then obviously you will have to consider new plumbing for it. Nevertheless, do try to site it as near to the soil stack as possible.

Other fittings can be repositioned more easily, but remember that they will have to be connected to both supply and waste pipes and, as well as being ugly, long runs of pipework are inefficient. Ideally, water waste should be carried in short pipe runs with as few bends as possible. Water supply pipes should also be kept short because the further hot water has to travel, the more heat it loses on the way. Siting the sanitaryware on one or two walls, rather than three or four, is also a good idea, as it can reduce the cost of the plumbing.

If the pipes are being boxed in—and that is by far the neatest way to deal with them—they should be individually lagged: the hot pipes to conserve energy and the cold ones to prevent condensation.

Other ways to hide pipes besides boxing them in include chasing them into the wall, routing them under the floorboards or constructing a false wall or half-wall.

Here are some guidelines for arranging fittings. Place the wc and bidet next to each other. Try not to position the wc where it would be in full view if the door were left open. Avoid putting the bath, wc or bidet under the window, because of draughts and lack of privacy. It is better not to put the basin there either because there is no convenient place for a mirror or bathroom cabinet, and splashes of soap and toothpaste will eventually spoil any blind or curtain.

If it is impossible to leave the window area clear, double glazing will cut out draughts. And, if you don't mind losing natural light, the lower panes of glass can be covered with mirror to give privacy, a reflection where it is needed and an easy-to-clean surface.

When you're arranging the fittings on the floor plan you'll probably find you have to overlap the user spaces in order to get everything in. This won't matter except where two people will be using the bathroom at the same time, at twin basins for example, in which case the maximum amount of elbow room will be needed. If space is limited, you can do some practical experiments to see if the user space can be reduced at all. Simply do the actions appropriate to the particular space using a piece of newspaper cut to size as a guide.

While you're working out the arrangement, try to imagine how easy the new bathroom will be to clean. Pipework has

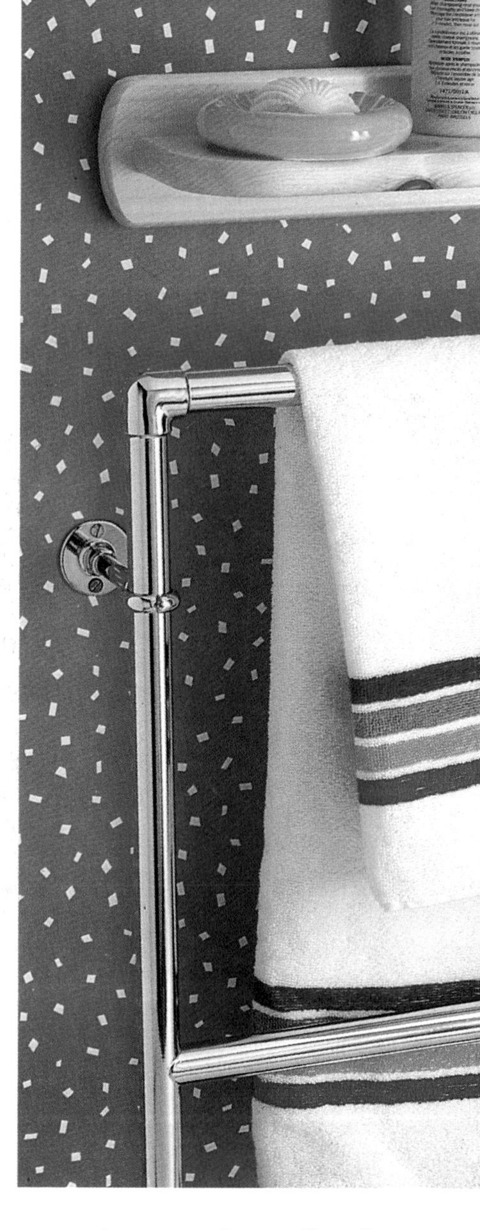

an amazing propensity to collect dirt, so, to side-step the problem, conceal it behind a false wall, box it in or hide it under the floorboards. This will look neater and make decorating simpler, too. The floor should be easy to vacuum or mop, with no awkward corners that have

to be swept or washed by hand. Windows should be accessible enough for you to polish without too much stretching.

Before you draft your final layout, give some thought to heating and ventilation, and also lighting, as these could all affect your plans.

Heating and ventilation

Condensation is the greatest bathroom bugbear. It ruins decorations, makes the atmosphere clammy and damp, and encourages mould growth on shower curtains, tile grouting and anywhere else it can get a foothold, creating a musty smell.

As it is caused by warm, moisture-laden air meeting a cold surface, the only way to eliminate condensation is to improve heating and ventilation. This may seem a contradiction in terms, especially as we have just suggested double glazing the window to stop draughts, but there is a difference. Ventilation is intended and controllable, while draughts are arbitrary. By making sure there is always enough ventilation to keep the air circulating, with the potential to step it up when the atmosphere is really steamy, you will solve at least half the problem.

Ventilation can be provided naturally by a window which is left ajar most of the time and which may be opened wide when necessary. Or it can be provided mechanically by an extractor fan.

A fan may be electric or non-electric; and either wall-mounted, ceiling-mounted or fitted into a single- or double-glazed window. Wall-mounted fans involve cutting a hole in the wall, while window-mounting means cutting the glass. A ceiling-mounted fan uses ducting through the loft to a grille in the eaves. The powered type is most efficient and can be unobtrusively flush-fitting, tile-sized and/or pastel-coloured.

For safety, an electric extractor must be operated by a pull-cord or a switch outside the room or, in a windowless bathroom, it can work automatically, coming on with the light and then running for a specific period after the light is switched off.

A warm room, apart from being a lot nicer to undress in, is less likely to suffer from condensation. Sudden temperature changes tend to aggravate the problem, so it is much better to provide a constant background heat which warms the structure. This background warmth need not be very great—just enough to take the

Below right: A bathroom cabinet that incorporates a row of film-star type bulbs makes a well-lit place for shaving or applying make-up. The slight heat they give out will help to prevent the mirror from steaming up. Far right: Fully enclosed downlighters recessed into the top of a bathroom vanity unit give problem-free lighting in a damp, steamy atmosphere.

chill off. If you have central heating, put a radiator in the bathroom, and fit it with a thermostatic valve so you can lower the heat a little when the bathroom is not being used. For all-year-round warmth, a towel rail connected to the hot-water circuit is best.

To boost the heat when the bathroom is being used, a permanently fixed gas or electric heater can be installed. Gas heaters must have a balanced flue and be fixed to an outside wall. Electric heaters must be wired to a fused connection (ordinary socket outlets are taboo in bathrooms) and placed out of reach of anyone using the bath or shower. A pull-cord switch is essential. Never take a portable heater into the bathroom—it is potentially lethal.

Lighting

Well-thought-out lighting will make the bathroom safer and more attractive. For safety reasons all fittings must be enclosed to render them waterproof and to prevent accidental contact with any live part.

For general light, surface-mounted fittings enclosed by an opalescent shade give a soft, pleasant light. Recessed downlighters give a uniform wash of light, but take care to position them so the beam doesn't flare off the mirror or shiny surfaces. In a windowless room, an illuminated ceiling guarantees all-over brightness or, for a more interesting and glamorous effect, choose enclosed wall lights.

For shaving and applying make-up, fluorescent strips concealed behind the mirror at the top and sides light up your face, not the glass, and the slight heat they generate keeps the mirror from misting up. A film-star style mirror framed or flanked with rows of bulbs does the same job but with more pzazz. Some bathroom cabinets incorporate lights and shaver points as well, taking care of three planning problems at once.

Shaver points are the only sockets which are allowed in a bathroom and must include an isolating transformer in order to virtually eliminate any danger of electric shock.

CHAPTER 10

A place for everything

For most people the main problem with re-vamping or re-fitting a bathroom is how to fit everything into too small a space. Here are some solutions.

Right: Fitted bathroom units are an attractive way to provide storage. The ones shown here have laminated fronts, with a choice of handles to match the sanitaryware. Facing page: Small-size sanitaryware like this basin is useful in a cramped space. The fact that it is wall-mounted means the user spaces can be overlapped to a greater degree.

In the majority of bathrooms it is hard enough to squeeze in all the equipment and still leave room for people, without having to make way for storage as well. But unless you are going to run your home like a hotel and provide each member of the family with his own sponge bag and towel, to be carried to and from the bathroom on each visit, space must be found.

However, if accommodating all the paraphernalia of bathtime is difficult, it should be viewed as just part of the much broader issue of making maximum use of the available space.

If you're creating a new bathroom from scratch, there are a couple of ways you can expand what you have.

Enlarging the room

The first possibility is to enlarge the room by extending into the hall, the landing or a neighbouring bedroom where there is sufficient under-used space for a few square metres not to be missed. This may be a question of simply moving a partition wall, or it could involve changing the positions of windows, doors and radiators and re-routing electric wiring and water pipes. Taking over part of the landing might even mean having to change the position of the hatch leading into the loft. Only you can decide whether the gains are worth the expense and disruption.

If by adding on to the existing bathroom the total area becomes great enough to split into two small ones—one en-suite, the other for general use—or one main bathroom with a separate shower room and/or lavatory next to it, the early morning traffic jam will be immediately halved. This is an improvement most would consider worth more than gold! The snag is that the storage problem might still remain unsolved, with the clutter simply spreading over two bathrooms instead of one.

Small-size fittings

The second space-saving strategy is to put in small-size fittings. Conventional baths come as small as 1,212mm long, which is not conducive to luxurious soaking but does allow you to put a bath and a shower into just slightly more space than would be occupied by a standard-sized tub.

Sitz baths and soaking tubs—short, high-sided baths, often with a built-in seat allowing you to have water up to chest level—take up little floor space, but they are not as easy to climb in and out of, especially for the elderly.

Recently, extra-deep shower trays, which are suitable for bathing or showering, have become available. They're perfect for children but not so good for comfort lovers.

Surprisingly, a corner bath can also save space by making the best use of an awkwardly shaped room.

In the case of the wc, it is the projection—the measurement from the front of the seat to the back of the cistern—which is most important in a small bathroom. While the depth of the bowl varies by only a few millimetres from model to model, the choice of cistern can make a substantial difference to the amount of floor area the complete unit occupies.

Generally, wash-down cisterns take up less space than the syphonic type, and you can buy special slim-line ones which are only 114mm deep.

Tiny hand basins, designed for cloakrooms, can be used in bathrooms too but they really will only be suitable for washing hands. Hair washing will have to be done in or over the bath with a shower mixer. Depending on the design you choose, these little basins can be wall-mounted on the flat or in a corner, set into a narrow shelf or vanitory unit, or recessed into the wall for the minimum projection.

Other strategies

If you are re-vamping rather than stripping and refitting your bathroom, there are other ways to capitalize on space. Simplest of all is to replace ordinary bath taps with a bath-shower mixer which will speed things up in the mornings and allow two different washing activities in the space of one fitting.

To save floor area inside the room, the door could be re-hung to open outwards; but before you do this, check that anyone dashing out of the bathroom won't hit an innocent passer-by!

If you're prepared to take drastic measures, the door could be moved to a more convenient spot. Windows could be re-positioned, or the airing cupboard demolished, with the hot-water tank being re-located in an adjacent bedroom or landing cupboard.

Storage suggestions

Having made available every centimetre of space, now is the time to find places to put all the things that need to be kept in the bathroom. The amount of storage you need depends largely on how many cupboards there are outside of the room. For example, if the airing cupboard is already in a bedroom or on the landing,

Above and right: In this bathroom, every bit of space has been used. Boxing off the bath with sliding doors instead of a panel creates space for storing unsightly items such as cleaning materials. An inset section in the wall has been created by constructing a simple framework of softwood battens with chipboard over the top, which has then been tiled. The glass shelves set into the tiled alcove can display some of the more attractive bathroom accessories.

or if you have a proper linen chest, you won't have to find a home for newly laundered sheets and towels.

(Incidentally, the airing cupboard is not the ideal place for long-term storage of household linen as the fabric will eventually yellow along the folds due to the constant warmth. It is much better to use the cupboard for airing linen and clothes in regular use.)

If spare soaps, toilet rolls and disposable nappies are kept elsewhere and if make-up, hair accessories and the laundry basket can be banished to the bedroom, it will ease the situation enormously. If not, then they will have to be accommodated as neatly and stylishly as possible.

The items to be stored can be divided into two groups: things in constant use and supplies. Those items used all the time must be kept handy, close to where they're needed. Spares and supplies can be put right away, out of sight if possible.

Near the basin, you'll need soap, shaving tackle, toothbrushes, toothpaste, tooth mugs and any other dental care products, nail scissors and manicure equipment, face cloths and towels. By the bath you'll have to have more soap (a separate bar is vital or you'll be constantly hopping out of the tub to retrieve it from the basin), bath oil, bath salts, deodorant, talc, pumice stone and other pedicure equipment, bath toys, a sponge, loofah, back brush, another nail brush and more towels. Shampoo and conditioner may stay by the basin or by the bath according to your preference. Convenient storage must also be found for cleaning materials, medicines, baby-care equipment and make-up.

Accessories and shelving

It is easy to dump things on the nearest surface, but in no time the cistern, bath rim and window sill will be littered, and you won't be able to find anything in the muddle.

To bring order to the chaos, rationalize. There are endless matching collections of bathroom accessories to choose from with racks to hold everything from toothpaste to toilet rolls. They can be made from plastic, Perspex, wood, glass, china, porcelain, chromium plate or brass in a vast array of designs. They can be free-standing or wall-mounted, even down to the tissue box cover. Wall-mounted accessories are better where space is limited but do be careful to fix them securely. Nothing looks sadder than fittings that are coming adrift from the wall. Also, especially in the case of towel rails, position them where they won't be used as makeshift grab-rails; they are not designed to take the strain.

If none of the ready-made ranges appeals, you can improvise to get the storage system you need. For the bath, fit a narrow shelf to the wall running the length of the bath and at least 500mm above it. A similar shelf above the basin is useful, but make sure it is not so deep or low that you bump your head on it every time you wash your hair.

A false wall about 900mm high, built round one or two sides of the room, conceals pipework and cisterns and provides a stretch of continuous shelf space at the same time. Where there is a complete false wall, shelves can be recessed into it, avoiding pipework.

Left: Many ranges of matching bathroom accessories are available today, in styles to suit any décor. Pine looks especially nice with primary colours.

Cabinets and cupboards

Traditionally, a mirror-fronted cabinet provides the main source of bathroom storage. If it is placed over the basin, make sure it isn't a potential hazard. The best cabinets are tall and wide rather than deep, with shallow shelves so all the contents can be seen easily. An open shelf below is useful for parking things like razors, make-up and contact lens gear while you are using them, and a section which is lockable is essential for keeping medicines.

The space under the basin can be put to good use by boxing it in to make a cupboard or by fitting a purpose-made vanitory unit with a drop-in basin. A cheaper alternative would be to make a framework round the basin, fix curtain track round the edge and hang pretty fabric curtains to screen low-level storage and ugly pipework.

If there's a gap between the end of the bath and the wall, this could be boxed in and given a hinged lid or drop-down front to make a laundry box, toy box or place to keep cleaning materials and spare toilet rolls. If there are no obstructions on the wall above this area, a ceiling-tall cupboard or shelf unit could be built.

Where the bath fits exactly along a short wall, shelves could be fixed behind it at the backrest end. In this situation, too, if there is the headroom, cupboards could be fixed over the bath. The things in them would be accessible only with the aid of a step-stool but they would be perfect for spare towels and bulk-bought supplies. Louvred doors would provide

Right: A small bathroom can be made to look larger with the right décor. A soft colour used throughout, a minimum of pattern and a good-sized mirror will work wonders.

enough ventilation to prevent steam damage.

The elegant fitted storage furniture designed specifically for bathrooms is beginning to catch on, but it is still very expensive. A similar effect could be achieved by installing kitchen units and decorating them with paint effects like marbling, stencilling or ragging to make them blend with the gentler bathroom environment.

Other storage ideas

Other kitchen storage ideas that could be transplanted are the wire wall grids with their various accessories, under-shelf baskets, plastic vegetable racks, tiered hanging baskets, pedal bins and storage jars.

There are a number of ways you can cure miscellaneous clutter. *For bath toys:* mesh bags hung from hooks over the bath or plastic baskets on nearby shelves. *For towels:* plenty of rails, firmly fixed and, where possible, over a radiator. If you can't get the length you want, buy a wooden curtain pole and cut it to the right size. *For bathrobes, face cloths, loofah mits and hand towels:* a row of coat pegs, at head height for the robes and waist height for the rest; stitching on loops of tape will stop them slipping off the hook. *For baby equipment:* a small trolley which travels between bathroom and nursery while the baby is small and can be put to good use in other rooms when he or she grows up.

Decorating to create space

If the room still looks cramped, you can always decorate it to give a feeling of space. Mirror is the perfect medium. Cover an entire wall with it, in sheet or tile form, and fix it along the bath panel to open up the floor area. Choose your wall carefully—you don't want to reflect the underpinnings of your plumbing or have to cut round a light switch.

Choose the mirror carefully, too. Ask for the steam-resistant kind and, if you want a warm and flattering reflection, a peach or pink tint. Mirrored doors on a wall of built-in cupboards have a similar effect.

If you hate to see your reflection everywhere you turn, mirror-mosaic breaks up the picture. Foil wallpaper will reflect the light but not you, and it looks particularly striking in a small room. When you hang it, take care to trim round the light switch rather than tucking it underneath. If the foil comes into contact with live wires, the result could be lethal.

Pale colours always make a room seem airy and spacious but they can make it insipid too. By painting the skirting board, and picture rail if there is one, a stronger tone of the same colour, you'll give the scheme impact and emphasize the horizontals, visually pushing back the walls. Wallpaper borders applied at ceiling, skirting and dado height do the same job.

A light-coloured wallpaper patterned with a tracery of flowers can be used over the walls and ceiling to give the room a cool, bowery atmosphere. A darker, richly patterned paper used in the same way will give a feeling of intimacy, but this can only work well where the room is perfectly neat. Clutter would make it claustrophobic.

Too many different colours, patterns and textures will fragment a small or busy room; it is much better to stick to one main colour throughout. If you would rather have all wallpaper than all tiles, protect it round the bath by covering with clear acrylic sheets screwed to the wall.

At floor level, continuing the carpet or tiles up the bath panel will give an illusion of space. Also, an imposing fixture like an airing cupboard will seem less dominant if it is painted or wall-papered to match the walls.

Above left: The same muted tiles have been used on the floor, walls and bath panel in this bathroom, in a colour that tones with the sanitaryware. The result is a peaceful, spacious-looking room. The stronger toning colour of the fittings and border tiles, together with the white taps and accessories, provides enough interest to prevent the effect from being monotonous or insipid.
Above: Using the same carpet up the sides of the bath, and matching it to the sanitaryware, makes a bathroom look bigger.

CHAPTER 11

Finishing lines

Bathroom surfaces have to combine practicality with good looks, surviving steam, splashes and even the occasional drenching without looking the worse for wear.

An attractive bathroom will only keep its good looks if all its components are up to their job. While you would expect the fittings to fulfil the purpose for which they were designed, the suitability of the coverings for the walls, floor and ceiling is not so clear-cut.

Bathroom surfaces generally must withstand water and steam, be easy to clean, present no safety risk and help to check condensation. The extent to which any material can measure up to these requirements is limited. And in any case, how essential each of the requirements is depends on your lifestyle, bathing habits and who will use the bathroom.

For instance, if you are dealing with a family bathroom to be used by two or more children under ten and at least one adult who is at home all day, you'll need tougher, more waterproof surfaces than would, say, a working couple with no children.

Ventilation makes a difference too. If the bathroom is regularly thick with steam, every surface must have a high resistance to humidity. But in a well heated and aired room, where care is taken to avoid a build up of steam, more delicate materials can be used.

Walls

The kind of wall covering you choose can either reduce condensation or make it worse. But before you decide on a particular covering in the hope that it will improve things, check that the dampness really is due to condensation and not penetrating damp.

If the dampness appears in cold, dry weather, then it is likely to be condensation; if it appears on a ceiling or outside wall and is much worse during or after rain, then it is probably penetrating damp. A more positive test can be done by drying out the damp patch with a heater, then sticking a piece of glass over it and sealing the edges with adhesive tape. After a few days, if the conditions are right, moisture will appear on the glass. If the moisture is on the side nearest you, it is condensation; if it is on the side nearest the wall, it is penetrating damp and must be cured by carrying out the necessary external repairs before any of the decorating can actually go ahead.

When it comes to choosing wall-coverings, look at the different areas you are dealing with very carefully. The walls around the shower, just above the bath and behind the basin are most exposed to moisture and must be protected with a waterproof surface. Other walls, out of splashing range, need not be so robust.

Below: Having to use water-resistant wall coverings in a bathroom needn't restrict your décor. Here textured tiles combine beautifully with vinyl wallpaper and tongue-and-groove cladding on the sloping ceiling. Painted wood battens which echo the tile grouting provide the finishing touch.

Below: Mosaic tiles, which are bought and fitted in sheets, give a dramatic look to a bathroom. The effect is accentuated by the use of no other colour but plain white.

Ceramic tiles
For wet areas, ceramic tiles are hard to beat. They come in all shapes and sizes, plain and patterned and, if waterproof adhesive and grouting are used, they are virtually impervious.

Tiles offer plenty of scope for imaginative decorating too. Look at ranges that include integrated designs with plain, patterned and border tiles, all co-ordinated to give the maximum decorative freedom. Some manufacturers make painted tiles which can be assembled on the wall to make a mural, while others will design tiles to your specifications.

Plain white tiles are cheapest but, unless you want a completely white scheme (which is tremendously chic but wouldn't last a week in a family of children and rugby players), they can look clinical. You can still take advantage of the bargain by relieving the austerity with coloured grouting or a border of decorated tiles. Patterned tiles dotted amongst the plain at random would add interest, but unless it is cleverly done by someone with an eye for composition it can look a bit too haphazard.

Mosaic tiles give a similar but more unusual effect. The individual tiles can be laid separately to form designs, but that is a lengthy and difficult job. It is much simpler and quicker to buy sheets of mosaic which can be laid complete relatively quickly.

Vinyl tile effects and laminates
If you like the look of tiling but don't want to go to any great trouble or expense, one of the new extra-thick vinyl wallcoverings embossed and patterned to look like tiles is an alternative to consider. This material is hung like wallpaper and can be cut with scissors or a sharp knife, so it is easy to negotiate any fixtures. It is completely waterproof and can be used in a shower enclosure, but the joins between strips must be properly sealed or moisture could seep through and eventually detach it from the wall. As the surface is comparatively warm to the touch, it provides some insulation, reducing the severity of condensation.

Panels of plastic laminate, plain or patterned, will also make an impervious bath or shower surround but, again, any seams must be properly sealed. In the wet zones less durable surfaces like wallpaper or paint can be covered with sheets of clear acrylic, Perspex or glass to give them splash-resistant protection.

Luxury look
For a look of luxury, and a price to match, mirror or marble could be used. Neither is completely resistant to the most extreme bathroom conditions—marble is inclined to stain and mirror can be affected by steam—but you would not

use such materials in an area where durability was the first priority.

Any of these water-resistant surfaces could be used over the entire wall area, and in a small or heavily used bathroom this would be desirable.

In a less than strictly functional bathroom, the walls not immediately adjacent to the splash areas could be covered with any of a number of surfaces, opening up the decorative options even further.

Paint and vinyl wallcovering

Paint is the cheapest and easiest to apply. Use vinyl silk, eggshell or a special anti-condensation paint. For a more interesting result, distress the paint to give a stippled, ragged or dragged finish or, if you wield a deft brush, try marbling, or painting a mural or a trompe l'oeil.

Vinyl wallcovering stands up well to a steamy atmosphere and offers the greatest choice of colours, patterns and, to a certain extent, textures, often with matching fabric and blinds to complete your scheme.

Wallboards, panelling and cork

Wallboards—which are made from hardboard, painted and lacquered to look like tiles, hessian or wood panelling—are fixed to the wall via battens, making a convenient and not too costly cover-up for poor plaster.

Below left: It's often possible to match tiles to fittings, as manufacturers make them to co-ordinate with the most popular colours of sanitaryware, and you can also get accessories in the same shades. Below right: Tiles in contrasting colours can create quite striking effects.

Below: Sealed cork flooring is very suitable for the bathroom and can also be used up the side of the bath and even on other surfaces like scales or a bin. Wicker baskets and house plants tie in very well with the natural texture of the cork.

If you would prefer the real thing, tongue-and-groove boards or wood panelling can be used to hide rough walls and pipes, or just because it looks handsome. To protect it from moisture, the surface should be very carefully varnished, sealed or painted.

Cork is one of the best general surfaces for a bathroom. It is pleasantly warm to the touch and seems to survive well in a damp atmosphere. Ready-sealed cork tiles have better water resistance than the natural wallcovering quality.

Wallboarding, wood panelling and sealed cork can all be used in the bath area if not too much water is being splashed around but they won't stand up to frequent drenching and should not be used in a shower cubicle.

Floors

A bathroom floor covering is expected to have many qualities. First and most important it must be safe, then it must be water-resistant, comfortable and easy to clean.

Vinyl sheet and tiles

The material that fulfils most of these requirements is vinyl sheet. If you buy the extra-wide, cushioned type, it gives a smooth, soft, fairly warm surface. Although the material itself is impervious, water could seep down around the edge; but by continuing the vinyl up on to the bath panel and curving it over an edging of scotia moulding round the skirting board, you will solve this problem.

Properly laid, vinyl tiles will provide just as good a surface and may be preferable in a small room, where sheet flooring would be difficult to handle and wasteful to fit.

Ceramic floor tiles

Ceramic tiles are water-resistant, easy to clean and, if there is under-floor heating, quite comfortable, too. However, their great drawback is that they can be slippery, especially when wet, and if you fall, you'll have a hard landing. Special non-slip floor tiles are much safer.

Tiles are very heavy so, before they are laid, check that the sub-floor can take the weight. If you want to have matching tiles throughout the room, use floor tiles on the walls; never the other way round, as wall tiles are rarely durable enough.

Mosaic can be used for floors very successfully, and when combined with mosaic walls as part of a total scheme the effect is very opulent.

If vinyl and ceramic floors seem practical but rather unyielding, a soft bath mat with a non-slip backing will make it more comfortable for bare feet.

Cork and rubber

Other smooth floors that are not so cold underfoot are cork tiles, suitably sealed or waxed, and rubber. Due to the influence of hi-tech, the latter is now quite readily available in white, black and mostly primary colours with studded or ribbed surfaces.

Carpet

Less practical but by far the most comfortable kind of bathroom floorcovering is carpet. It is warm, soft and perfectly safe but not easy to keep clean; and once wet, it takes a long time to dry.

Unless you belong to a family of very restrained bathers, buy carpet that is made specifically for the bathroom. Both pile and backing will be synthetic—probably nylon, polyester or polypropylene—as natural fibres rot in moist, warm conditions. Avoid carpet with foam backing, which will soak up the water, keeping the pile unpleasantly soggy and perhaps damaging the sub-floor. If possible, loose-lay the carpet so it can be taken up or at least rolled back if it does get wet.

Carpet tiles are normally loose laid and can be washed and dried if necessary. As with any tiles, they have the advantage of being very economical in a small, awkwardly shaped area. The manufacturers suggest that you shuffle the tiles round from time to time to equalize wear, but in a bathroom this may be difficult as so many of them will have been cut to fit.

Left: Carpet can be used in the bathroom provided both the pile and the backing are synthetic, and it is not foam-backed. It gives a warm, luxurious look that offsets any clinical atmosphere. Below: Ceramic tiles are a practical floor covering for the bathroom, being water-resistant, easy to clean and durable. A simple slatted bathmat of duck board looks good against the smooth surface of the tiles.

Not, strictly speaking, carpet but still a very pleasing pile floor covering, the shaggy cotton twist material normally used for bath mats can be bought in larger quantities to cover the whole floor area. It comes in a whole spectrum of colours and, even if none suits you perfectly, cotton is easy to dye.

Windows

The window is a strong decorative feature in any room and the bathroom need be no exception. The style of bathroom and the tastes of its occupants will decide whether a neat and practical window dressing or something more flamboyant is appropriate.

If a window is not overlooked at all, it could be left bare with patterned, etched or stained glass providing the necessary feeling of security.

The next simplest treatment is a blind. Venetian and roller blinds are both crisp-looking and practical and come in colours

Above: A suspended ceiling can turn a cold, box-like bathroom into a warm and cozy retreat. A translucent screen with fluorescent tubes behind it creates a dramatic effect that complements the slatted ceiling. Right: A festoon blind turns a window into an elegant focal point, and the symmetrical arrangement of the bathroom fittings enhances the effect.

to match any scheme. To get privacy without sacrificing too much daylight, fix a roller blind upside down so the roller part is on the sill and the blind is pulled up as far as necessary then anchored on hooks that are screwed to the sides of the frame.

For a slightly softer touch, hang a roller blind as usual, then, from fabric, make a stiffened, prettily shaped pelmet to frame the top and sides of the window. The blind and pelmet could be made from the same fabric or from a patterned one with matching plain material.

Another way to get a more dramatic effect using roller blinds is to hang two together. Fix a lace one nearest the glass and a fabric one in front, then pull them down to different levels so their shaped lower edges echo each other.

Gentler still, Roman and festoon blinds are a pretty fabric treatment for windows where you don't want curtains.

Louvred shutters are an attractive summery way to screen windows. The two-tier, bi-fold ones with tilting louvres are best as they give you complete control over the amount of light you let in.

Curtains can add the necessary prettiness to a plain room. Café curtains hung across the lower part of the glass let in most light, while heavy lace or fine muslin ones diffuse it beautifully. Short frilled curtains or, in a large bathroom, floor-length drapes with tie backs, turn the window into the most important feature.

Ceilings

The paint or vinyl wallcovering used for the walls is perfectly suitable for the ceiling too, but remember that bathroom ceilings are exposed to the full effects of steam. So, to give whatever decorative material you choose the best chance of survival, make sure ventilation is adequate.

Sometimes when a bathroom is the result of partitioning a large room in an older house, the ceiling is too high in relation to the walls. You can reduce the height visually by painting the ceiling and the top of the walls above the picture rail a darker colour. By putting a wooden fascia board round the room at the level you would, in a perfect world, prefer the ceiling to be, fitting fluorescent tubes behind it and then painting the upper part of the walls and ceiling dark, the top of the room will effectively disappear.

Another method is to make a suspended ceiling using panels of slatted wood which are hung from chains attached to hooks screwed into the joists. A suspended ceiling made up of translucent plastic panels can be top-lit with fluorescent tubes for a cheerful brightness.

If the room is so lofty that it never warms up properly, it would be better to lower the level of the ceiling permanently. This can be done by making a false plasterboard ceiling. Add decorative coving to make it look more established. A false ceiling made from tongue-and-groove cladding is within the scope of most diy enthusiasts. If the sauna look of the pine doesn't go with your décor, paint it as for any other woodwork.

CHAPTER 12

Suite dreams

The fittings are the most important components of a new bathroom. Choose them with an eye to the future, planning the layout to allow for every eventuality.

Right: Modern ranges of sanitaryware come in some lovely colours, which you can carry through in your choice of flooring, tiles, curtains, towels, soap dishes and other accessories.

More than any other furniture, bathroom fittings once they are installed become fixtures, and will remain long after you have changed the décor.

There are five main pieces of equipment to include—the bath, basin, wc, bidet and shower. Whatever the size of your bathroom, it is much better to aim for as many of them as you can fit into the space, since additions or changes made later will be expensive and disruptive.

This doesn't mean you should cram the room full—just decide what you need, then look for fittings in sizes and shapes that will make a pleasing, comfortable arrangement while providing all the facilities you need. If it is impossible to incorporate everything you want, make the best of your limited space by buying the best and most beautiful of the essentials.

Try to select all the fittings from one range, as the related shapes will make the room look more integrated. Sometimes you'll find that a single manufacturer does not make everything you need—for example, the range may include an acrylic bath but not a cast iron one, or a pedestal basin and no vanitory sink. If this happens, hunt around until you find complementary shapes that will mix together happily.

If you are choosing coloured fittings, remember these are influenced by fashion, and the shades available change over the years. A little while ago, dark colours like sepia, burgundy and midnight blue were very popular but now the trend is towards softer pastels and neutrals such as champagne, Indian ivory and Kashmir beige. The core of standard colours, which includes avocado, pampas, cameo pink and Alpine blue, is available in most ranges while some of the fashion colours are limited to certain manufacturers and products. Matching

tiles are available for many of the most popular colours.

When you select a colour, don't be too influenced by current trends. Your own preference is much more important—you'll have to live with it for a long time. As a guide, dark colours look sophisticated but show hard water marks and ought to be dried thoroughly after use to keep them looking good. Distinctive colours are fine if they are your particular favourite but could look dated and be difficult to decorate around in years to come. Neutrals are infinitely versatile and easy to live with, while white is a classic and the interior designers' choice.

Whatever colour you choose, even if it is white, check that all the fittings match exactly. Sometimes there are colour variations between those made from different materials or by different manufacturers, and even a slight change will be noticeable.

Bathtubs

The standard bath is rectangular, 1,700mm long and 700mm wide with taps at one end, but there are plenty of variations.

Small baths for tiny spaces have already been mentioned, but there are also baths big enough for two, glamorous corner baths, reproduction Victorian tubs with claw feet and even oval, heart- or cloverleaf-shaped ones.

Inside, the tub can be contoured with integral ledges for soaps and sponges, with a sloping back and armrests for comfort; or shaped to follow the lines of the body, reducing the bath's capacity and hence the cost of a deep soak in hot water.

The taps are normally at one end together with the waste and overflow, but they can be positioned on a corner or side instead, within easy reach of the recumbent bather. The waste can be a plug and chain or the neater knob- or lever-controlled pop-up type. The bath may be drilled with one, two or three holes depending on the style of taps you want or, if you prefer wall mounted taps, you can order an undrilled bath.

Hand grips are useful for climbing in and out, and a flat, non-slip base is a desirable safety feature, which is essential if you have an over-bath shower.

Most baths come with side panels and

Below left: Fittings are normally designed as a complete suite, and it's advisable where possible to choose all the pieces from the same range, especially with the more distinctive designs like this art nouveau suite.
Below: Bathtubs come in a wide range of shapes, styles and prices, including the corner bath and large rectangular bath shown here. Taps need not be positioned over the plug end.

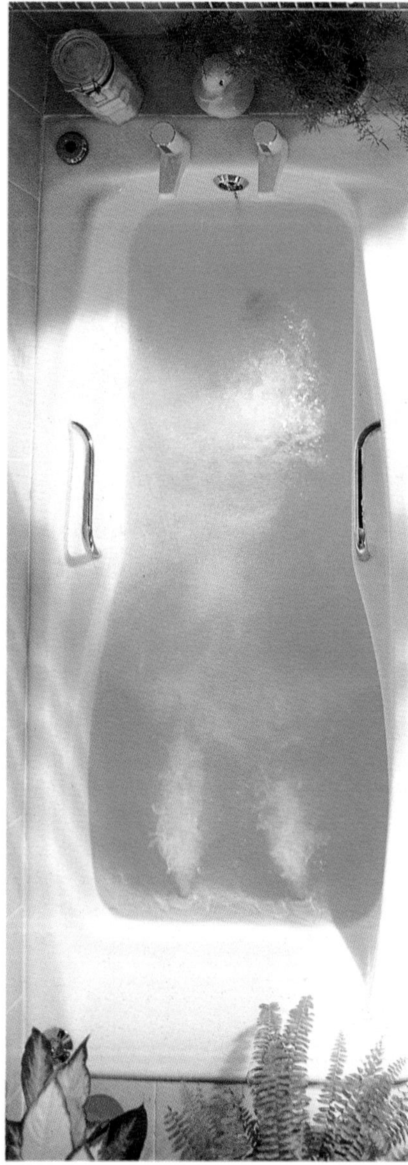

Above: In a whirlpool bath you can bathe while streams of aerated water invigorate your body and soothe your muscles. Special kits can convert an ordinary bath into a whirlpool.

sometimes end panels to conceal the underside of the bath and the pipework, but they must be removable for access to the plumbing. Panels are almost always made from plastic and are rarely attractive. If you prefer, a panel can be made from chipboard and covered with tiles, cork or some other decorative finish to match the rest of your scheme.

Baths are usually made from cast iron, pressed steel, acrylic or fibreglass. Each material has its share of advantages and shortcomings but you must weigh them up and decide which is best for your purposes.

Cast iron is the traditional material. It is durable with a lustrous, scratch-resistant surface, and it is rigid so it won't 'give' when you stand in it. It is also comparatively expensive and very heavy —something to be borne in mind if you live in a flat several floors up with no lift!

Pressed steel is fairly rigid with a vitreous enamel finish, and it is cheaper and lighter than cast iron.

Plastic, including acrylic and fibreglass, is light and warm to the touch and can be moulded into more complicated shapes than metal. It will not chip but is easily scratched, even by household cleaners, and is permanently damaged by cigaratte burns. Because they are so light, plastic baths are inclined to move and bend in use if not anchored securely during installation.

Most baths have a shiny surface and come in a range of plain colours, though recently the choice of finishes has broadened to include eggshell or silk surfaces and effects such as marble, pearlized and glitter finishes, colour shading and patterned decorations. Usually, the whole suite is decorated to match.

Another fairly new development is the introduction of whirlpool and air-jet baths. These are reputedly therapeutic and certainly pleasant and relaxing. Both are electrically operated and massage the bather by forcing air into the water to create jets of bubbles.

The difference between the two systems is that the whirlpool circulates the water, mixing it with air as it is pumped round; while air-jet baths, as you would expect, pump in air alone. The whirlpool is more expensive than the air-jet type, although sometimes an existing bath can be converted into a whirlpool, and this is much cheaper. Both baths can be used with or without the hydromassage system in operation.

Basins

The choice is between a pedestal, wall-hung or vanitory basin.

The pedestal basin is the type most often included as part of a suite. It is usually made from vitreous china with a matching hollow column which performs the dual task of concealing the pipework and giving some support to the basin. The standard height is 815mm, which may be on the low side for tall adults, but it is meant to suit all the family including children. If you live in an entirely adult household and would prefer a higher

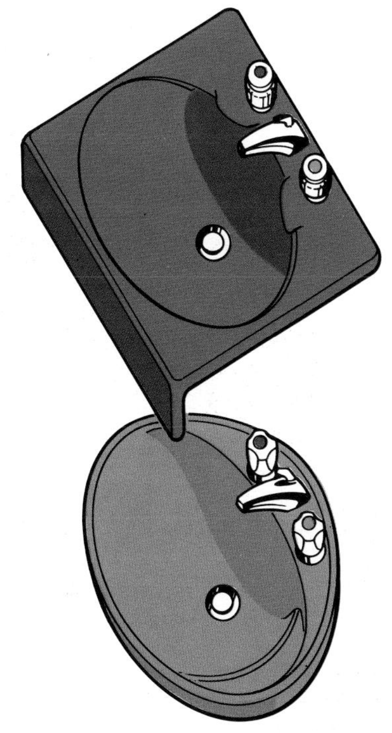

basin, the level could be raised by standing the pedestal on a plinth.

Wall-hung basins do not have this problem, as you can fix them at any level you like. Commonly made from vitreous china, these basins are supported on brackets attached to an outside or other load-bearing wall—partition walls are not really strong enough to take the weight. Because they leave the floor below clear, cleaning is easy. The only drawback is that the plumbing is very visible; however, you can make it less unsightly by fitting a chrome trap or choosing a basin with a special matching trap cover to conceal the pipework.

Vanitory or counter-top basins can be made from vitreous china, pressed steel, cast iron or plastic. Depending on the design, they can be set into a surface fitted under it or moulded in one to form an integral part of it. They are generally used with a vanitory unit, which provides cupboard space below and conceals all the pipework. Alternatively, the basin may be set into a deep shelf which has a fascia board to hide the pipes. This arrangement is especially useful if you want to sit at the basin and adjoining surface to, say, put on make-up, as there is knee-space underneath.

Standard sizes for basins are 635 by 455mm and 560 by 405mm, but this is academic since there are very many different sizes to choose from. The shapes available include oval, round, square, triangular and kidney- or shell-shaped. Choose the biggest basin you can accommodate and pick one with a good bowl shape—water tends to splash out of shallow ones.

Like baths, basins are available drilled with one, two, three or no tap holes, and the range of colours, finishes and patterns available is, if anything, greater.

Wc's

The old high-level cistern has virtually disappeared now and, apart from a few replacement ones and the reproductions made for nostalgia buffs, all modern wc's are compact low-level units.

The lavatory bowl is almost always made from vitreous china with a matching or plastic cistern. Although the basic shape remains the same, manufacturers modify it to match their various ranges of fittings.

There are two main types of wc—the wash-down and the syphonic. The wash-down type, which simply flushes the bowl with water, forcing the waste out, is cheapest though rather noisy. The more expensive syphonic type clears the bowl by suction and, at the same time, flushes it clean. The action is quieter but there is more risk of blockages.

With the wash-down type, the cistern is sometimes connected to the bowl by a

Far left above: A plain bath can be turned into something special by building an adjacent platform with steps at one end. Far left below: Modern basins and taps are available in a wide range of styles, such as this classic combination which would blend with any décor. Left: Square and oval basins make a striking alternative to the more usual shape but you should make sure they are practical to wash in as well as good-looking. Above: The wc on the left of this picture is close-coupled, which means the cistern and bowl are directly linked. The one on the right of the picture has a length of pipe connecting the cistern and bowl, and it is a wash-down type, rather than syphonic (which are always close-coupled). The pipe on the bottom right of the picture is a flexible soil pipe connector, which makes fitting a new wc easier.

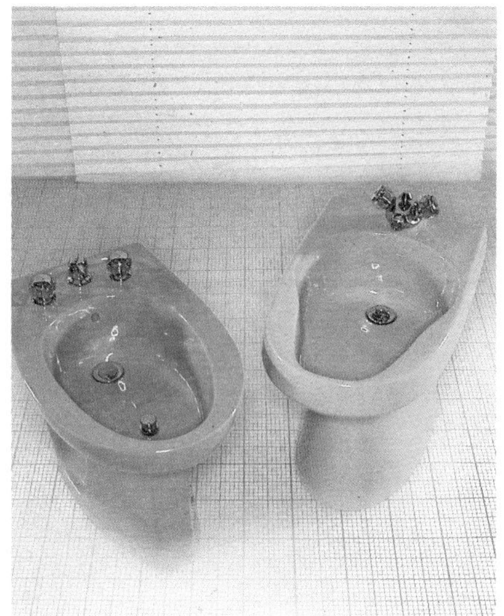

Right: A bidet is a useful, hygienic addition to the bathroom and can be matched to the rest of the sanitaryware. Above: The bidet on the left of this picture has a spray fitted at the base of the bowl, while the bidet on the right does not, and works instead like a hand basin. Far right: These two pictures show how ascending spray and rim-supply bidets work.

length of pipe. A neater alternative is the close-coupled cistern, which is mounted at the back of the pan with no gap between the two. Syphonic wc's are invariably close-coupled.

Neater still is the concealed cistern. Here, the cistern is hidden in a duct or false wall so all that is visible is the wc bowl and the flush lever or knob. The wc may be a floor-standing back-to-wall model or a wall-mounted cantilevered one. Both are more streamlined with fewer dust-collecting contours than the conventional suite.

Bidets

Another fairly recent addition to our bathrooms, the bidet is a valuable aid to personal hygiene and also useful for washing feet and soaking laundry. For convenience, place it next to the wc.

Bidets are made from vitreous china and can be bought as part of a bathroom suite or as an optional extra. They are divided into two main types according to their method of filling.

The first is the over-rim type which works like a wash basin, having pillar taps or a mixer which may incorporate a douche spray.

The second is the heated-rim type, which fills by flushing the water into the bowl from under the rim, sometimes with an ascending spray as well, and there are tap handles to control the temperature. This method serves to warm the edge of the bidet, making it more comfortable to sit on. In either case, the waste can be a plug and chain or pop-up.

The bidet can be floor-standing with an integral pedestal, a back-to-wall model or wall-hung from concealed brackets.

Showers

A shower saves time and money since it normally takes only one-fifth of the hot water needed for a bath. The two factors governing the type of shower you will have are its location and the method of heating water.

In a small bathroom, an over-bath shower may be the only choice. Protect the area around the bath by fitting a special fixed, hinged or folding screen made of plastic or safety glass, or a shower curtain.

Where there is enough floor space, a separate shower is preferable. This can be a shower tray built into a watertight tiled enclosure or fitted with a separate plastic or safety glass cubicle, or it can be a pre-fabricated cubicle all ready to plumb in.

Shower trays are made from porcelain enamelled cast iron, pressed steel, vitreous china, glazed fire-clay or moulded plastic, and some are designed with an upstand round two or three sides which is incorporated into the tiling to prevent leaks. The enclosure should be fitted with a wall-mounted soap dish at a convenient height and a door, screen or curtain to prevent water splashing into the room. You could also fit a grab handle and even a folding seat.

Pre-fabricated shower cubicles come complete with walls, tray, all the internal fittings and sometimes a door or screen

Left: One way of creating a shower is to fit it into a tiled enclosure, with a shower curtain, door or screen. Above: Shower trays are usually square or oblong and should have a slip-resistant finish.

Above: Another type of shower enclosure is the separate cubicle, made of safety glass, which fits on to a shower tray. There is a wide selection of doors available, so you can choose one to suit your layout. Right: If you don't have room for a separate one, a shower can be fitted above a bath. A shower curtain or screen makes it watertight. Here an instantaneous shower has been fitted, which heats up cold water from the rising main rather than using existing hot water supplies.

as well. They are usually made from moulded plastic.

If you have plenty of hot water, the shower can be fed from existing supplies using a bath-shower mixer, which diverts the flow from the taps to a flexible hose and hand set, or the more sophisticated independent built-in mixer. If you opt for the latter, choose one that is thermostatically controlled to give a flow of water at a constant temperature. This protects the person who is using the shower from being scalded should someone use cold water at the same time elsewhere in the house, thereby reducing the water pressure.

The shower head can be permanently fixed at shoulder or head height or it can be adjustable, being mounted on a sliding rail or on a choice of wall brackets.

In order to get a good spray instead of a miserable trickle, there must be an adequate head of water, which means having a vertical distance of at least 1 metre between the highest level of the shower spray and the base of the cold water tank. The greater the distance, the greater the pressure of spray. If the tank isn't high enough, you could either raise it by putting it on blocks, or install an electric pump to boost the pressure.

If you don't have a constant source of hot water near where you want to position the shower, an instantaneous gas or electric shower could be the answer. This is fed by the mains and heats the water as it passes through the unit. The temperature is, to a certain extent, decided by the volume of water, which means that you cannot have a hot, high-pressure shower. Any electric shower should be installed by a qualified electrician.

Bathroom taps

Taps and mixers for baths, basins and bidets are available in a variety of designs to suit the different styles of bathroom fittings, from Regency, Edwardian and Victorian reproductions to slick modern shapes. They are, in the main, made from brass, although some of the cheaper ones are all plastic. Brassware can be finished in chrome, gold, coloured epoxy or polished brass; plastic fittings are either coloured or chromed. Tap handles can match the body of the tap or be made from a decorative material such as enamel, onyx, glass or patterned china.

Pillar taps are the familiar separate hot and cold type with a knob or cross-head

handle. For mixer taps, the hot and cold water inlets are either together in one block with the spout and taps (called a monobloc), or they are separated. Sometimes the connecting piece is hidden so the mixer appears to be in separate parts.

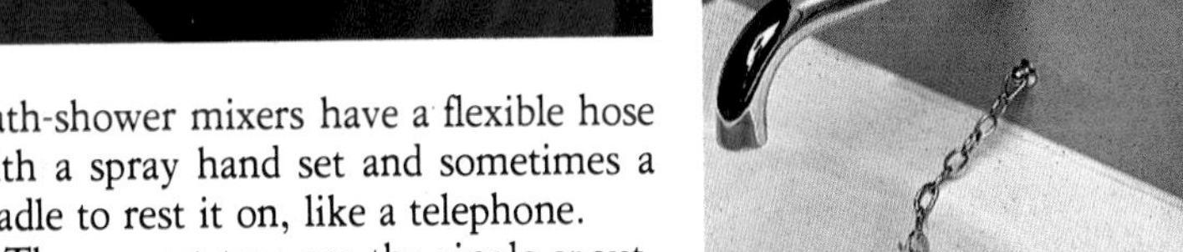

Bath-shower mixers have a flexible hose with a spray hand set and sometimes a cradle to rest it on, like a telephone.

The newest taps are the single spout, single lever type with one control to regulate both temperature and water flow.

Left: The six pictures on the left illustrate a selection of the bathroom taps that are available today. One type of basin mixer (top left) has separate holes for the hot and cold water inlets. The pop-up waste lever is often on the outlet spout. The other type of basin mixer, the monobloc (top right), is made in one piece. Many mixer taps have decorative plastic handles, as well as built-in plungers that control the pop-up waste. Bath-shower mixers (centre left and centre right) have a flexible hose with a spray handset. An adaptation of the monobloc (bottom left), this neat tap has just one hand wheel and a separate nozzle. The tap (bottom right) is a standard pillar tap. Above: These two pictures show a pop-up waste closed and also opened. When closed, a tight seal is created; once opened, water is released but the plug remains in the fitting.

CHAPTER 13

Splashing out in style

A distinctive style will give a bathroom personality and help detract from its shortcomings. Sanitaryware, accessories and surface treatments can all fit in with the theme.

Some of the character cameos suggested here for creating a particular effect are so simple they won't cost much to copy; others are for devoted scene setters.

Leafy conservatory

For summer all the year round, choose a predominantly green and white scheme with splashes of salmon pink—think of geraniums and you'll get the idea.

Paint the walls leaf green and cover them with garden trellis painted white or reverse the colours if you prefer. Tile the floor in white and one wall with mirror tiles to reflect the daylight.

Put white louvred doors on the cupboards and matching shutters at the window. If the window is not overlooked, the shutters could be exchanged for glass shelves fixed across it to make the perfect indoor garden for houseplants.

More plants can be suspended in hanging baskets or grouped around the bath, on the floor or on the surrounding ledge. Plants like *Impatiens, Nephrolepsis exaltata* and *Schefflera* love warm, humid conditions.

Keep bathroom clutter in baskets—natural or painted green or white. If there's room, a cane armchair with a fabric cushion looks comfortable and will survive the steam. Introduce the pink with towels and soaps, and stick to white or brass finishes for taps and accessories.

Feminine boudoir

Essentially feminine and deliciously luxurious, the boudoir is decked out in soft, delicate colours like pink, peach and cream. Textures are all important. The bathroom suite, if it is new, should be silk-finished rather than hard gloss. Fitted carpet, peach-tinted mirrors and diffused, glowing wall lamps are all conducive to the romantic atmosphere.

Use fabric lavishly with flouncy festoon blinds at the window and an extravagantly tented ceiling. A dressing table with a frilled skirt and matching stool is essential for make-up. If it can be set into an alcove, mirrors on three sides will give a clear, all-round view.

Keep the more basic signs of bathroom life in the background by putting the wc and bidet behind a partition out of sight of the bath and dressing table. Fit the bath into an alcove with curtains tied back at each side like a stage. Hang the curtains from a ceiling mounted track or a pole,

Above left: The 'leafy conservatory' style of bathroom features fresh green tones accented with salmon-pink, floral wallpaper and plenty of house plants. Cane furniture adds to the natural look. Above: A bath in an alcove with pretty curtains tied at the sides sets the scene for the feminine boudoir style. A dressing table is another essential, plus pretty wallpaper and soft, feminine colours.

attaching them with ribbons instead of rings. If there is no alcove, make one by enclosing the bath with built-in floor to ceiling cupboards at each end.

If the bath curtains also have to act as shower curtains, line them with thin plastic. If the waterproof linings are detachable, you will be able to wash the two separately.

Finishing touches in this bathroom would be glass bowls of pastel-coloured soaps, pot-pourri to keep the air sweetly scented and, instead of a pull-cord switch for the light, a silky cord with a tassel.

Morning fresh

Light, bright and lively is the atmosphere in a bathroom that makes you glad to wake up. White fittings and primary colours look clean and fresh. Choose one brilliant colour—red, yellow, green or blue—and use it exclusively. The taps, lavatory seat, door knobs, cupboard handles, and towels can all be colour-matched.

The look is crisp and efficient, so the floor should be smooth: tiles or vinyl, plain rather than patterned unless it is a stripe, spot or check. Walls are white—tiled or painted—with a bright-coloured border all round. A white roller blind at the window and lots of mirrors make the most of the daylight, and at night robust bulkhead lamps (intended for outdoors and therefore waterproof) with coloured casings provide illumination.

For storage, there could be open shelves with painted wicker or plastic baskets to keep things tidy. Roller blinds, plain or striped, pull down at the front to cover them.

Towels, facecloths and the bath mat are white or the primary colour, and accessories are simple shapes in plastic of the appropriate colour. A shower curtain could be in spinnaker nylon, sold for yacht sails, as bright as can be.

Hi-tech

If you like a bathroom to be a comfortable, peaceful place to lounge and linger in, then this look is not for you.

Stainless steel fittings set the style, along with chic Italian or Danish taps finished in black, white or stainless steel. Black studded rubber flooring is surprisingly comfortable underfoot and, again, the ships' chandler can be plundered for fittings to keep sponges (natural) and soaps (white) handy by the bath; use a thick white rope for a grab-rail or even a porthole for a window.

No colour is allowed to spoil the effect. Toothbrushes, shaving tackle, containers, everything must be black, white or metallic. Soften the effect with piles of fluffy towels in white, grey and black with just a dash of bright blue.

Wholesome sauna

This is not really a steam cabinet, but it has the same wholesome Scandinavian look. The materials in this kind of bathroom are natural, with pale wood panelling for the walls, cork or duck boarding for the floor and pinoleum blinds at the window. The fittings and tiles should be white, classic shapes and with no decoration. The taps, too, would be simple and finished in brass, chrome or white. The shower cubicle—and there would be a separate one—should be tiled throughout.

Pine or bamboo accessories are in

Facing page and below left: The 'morning fresh' bathroom style features clean white fittings and sanitaryware, accented by a vivid primary colour. Plenty of mirror space adds to the light, bright feeling. Below: Pine or other pale wood panelling is the crucial element in the sauna-like bathroom, combined with simple white fittings and tiles.

keeping with the natural look and would hold a selection of natural sponges, loofahs, pumice stones, pure bristle brushes and unperfumed toiletries.

A little wooden stool or a folding director's chair with a canvas seat would be the only extra furniture.

Victorian excess

Dark wood, brass and white porcelain give this bathroom a distinctly masculine and elegant flavour.

Below and right: White porcelain fittings, brass taps and rich, dark wood characterize the Victorian-style bathroom. Accessories must be in keeping as well, and arranging the bath so it projects into the room is also very much in the style of the period.

The fittings would be white—ideally, original Victorian or Edwardian pieces from an architectural salvage centre, with brass taps and shower fittings from the same source. If the right originals are not available, good reproductions could be substituted.

The bath side, the basin and even the wc could be boxed or built in with dark wood panelling. This really ought to be mahogany, but a lesser timber stained dark would give a similar effect. Mirrors in imposing wood frames should line the walls and marble panels protect the area around the bath. If there is space, the bath could project into the room, like a bed, and be panelled round three sides, with a broad ledge round the top. A low table placed at the end of the bath would keep books and magazines within reach of the bather. Tiles could be white or cream with a raised pattern border or dado rail to edge them.

The room should look comfortable, lived in and furnished with fitted carpet, an armchair and pictures on the walls. Accessories would be made from brass, glass or white china or a combination of those materials. Towels in masculine colours like maroon, navy and forest green, embroidered with a monogramme, and a collection of silver, tortoiseshell or ivory-backed brushes would complete the picture.

CHAPTER 14

Bright ideas

If new bathroom fittings are out of the question, don't despair. There are plenty of ways to improve what you've got, and they needn't cost you a fortune.

The price of a new bathroom is not inconsiderable, and if you live in a rented place, plan to move shortly or simply have a limited budget and more pressing priorities, it may be too big an investment to make. Here are some practical alternatives to a complete refit.

Cleaning up

If the fittings themselves have seen better days, clean them up and see if they're really as bad as you thought. Chrome polish from car accessory shops can bring the shine back to neglected taps, and lemon juice will sometimes remove hard water stains under taps, around plug holes and in the wc bowl. If this doesn't do the trick, try one of the proprietary bath-stain removers. These are very powerful chemicals, so read the instructions carefully and use as recommended. An old toothbrush and cream or paste cleaner will shift dirt trapped round the base of the taps and in the overflow.

Bath renovations

If the bath enamel is chipped, you may be able to repair it by using one of the special touch-up kits sold for the purpose. If the surface of a steel or cast iron bath is too far gone, the only answer (other than replacing it altogether) is to have it professionally re-surfaced. If you decide to try this, you may be offered the chance to change the colour at the same time; but if you do, remember that the bath will no longer match the other fittings.

If the bath is in reasonably good condition but still looks drab, some new taps might be all that is needed to brighten it up. Coloured ones look particularly cheerful.

An ill-fitting or split bath panel looks scruffy, so abandon it and box in the bath, giving it a wide wood or tiled ledge all round for a fitted look. Alternatively, you can add a touch of glamour by building one or two steps up to the bath right along the side, carpeting them and the bath side to match the floor. This gives a semi-sunken effect and, as a bonus, makes it easier to get in and out of the water.

If you have a very old bath, the type with a rounded tub and claw feet, remove the panel altogether. The underside of the bath will be dirty but if you clean it up, treating any rust spots, and paint it with aerosol car paint, it will look as good as new. If the pipework is ugly, paint it a dark colour so it recedes visually. (This type of bath is very fashionable now, and reproduction versions sell for fairly high prices. So don't write it off just because it's old-fashioned.)

Facing page: Very old bathtubs are often beautifully shaped and look very homely and cozy, especially with period furnishings. If the surface is in bad condition, it can be repaired or resurfaced for a whole new lease of life. Left: Boxing it in is one way of updating an old wc, and adding a bright new seat completes the transformation. Below: An under-basin unit gives you the chance to streamline your bathroom, hides the plumbing and provides useful storage.

Improving the wc

If the wc is old but not cracked or chipped, there is no reason to replace it. A grubby or cracked seat can be replaced either with a matching or contrasting plastic seat or with a wooden one.

High-level cisterns that still work well should stay put—if you decide to swap for a low level one, you may have to move the wc forward, away from the wall, to accommodate the new cistern, just giving yourself another set of problems.

Attractive ceramic or figured cast iron cisterns on decorative brackets can be renovated. Clean the ceramic thoroughly and treat the brackets and cast iron cistern for rust, then paint them.

Plastic cisterns are markedly unattractive but, boxed in with wood or plywood, and painted or papered to match the walls, they are far less unsightly. The chain could be replaced with a new brass one, and the tacky rubber pull swapped for a wood, china or glass one.

Ugly low-level cisterns can often be boxed in too, either behind a low false wall or into the lower part of a ceiling-high shallow cupboard. The cupboard space above the cistern can be fitted with shelves, making convenient storage space for spare toilet rolls, tissues and cleaning materials.

It's also possible to box in an old toilet bowl (along with the cistern if it's low-level). Add bright tiles and, if needed, a new seat to match your décor.

Clever cupboards

The basin can never look smart while there's a tangle of pipework clearly visible under it. Box it in to match the bath, incorporating if you can a flat surface around the bowl as parking space for jars and bottles. If the base becomes a cupboard, you're well on the way to

Above: Cheerful décor can brighten up a plain bathroom to an extraordinary degree. Right: There's no need to treat period-style fittings with too much respectful authenticity. Sometimes a lively, modern colour scheme works perfectly and creates a delightful new look.

having a much tidier, streamlined bathroom. Cupboard knobs to match the door handles and taps to match the bath will help make the room come together.

Renovating tiles

There's nothing like dingy tiles for making the whole bathroom look depressing. Try scrubbing the tiles first with floor and wall cleaner and then go over the grouting lines with an old toothbrush dipped in a strong bleach solution. If you like the colour or pattern of the tiles and if the grouting comes up white, this should be enough to give them a new lease of life. If the grouting is still discoloured you can remove it and re-grout in white or a colour, or just cover it with a skin of special tile grouting 'paint', which will bond with the grouting.

If you hate the tiles, you can paint over them with oil-based gloss or eggshell, preparing and priming the surface first, but this is not really satisfactory and should be seen as a temporary measure. For longer-lasting results, tile over the existing tiles with new ones.

If the tiles are in good condition and not too offensive, you can liven them up in a number of ways. Edge them with decorated border tiles in a complementary colour or design; stick a wallpaper border all round the tiled area to enclose it and perhaps link the tiles to the wallpaper or the fabric used for the curtains. Wooden moulding fixed along the edge of the tiles finishes them off nicely, and a border made from three or four rows of half-round wooden moulding, each painted a different shade, will add colour to an expanse of plain tiles.

Painting or papering the walls is an easy and not too expensive way to revamp the way a bathroom looks, but if the walls are in bad shape, tongue-and-groove cladding is cheaper than replastering. Natural wood is always attractive, but more interesting effects can be achieved by painting each board a different 'ice-cream' colour or by breaking up the wall area with stencilled borders.

If you don't want to go to the trouble or cost of panelling, bumpy walls can be disguised by hanging framed pictures over the whole area from skirting to ceiling. The pictures need not be very special—even a pretty soap wrapper becomes a work of art when it is framed. It is the volume that matters. If framing isn't possible, a collage of cartoons, newspaper headlines, fashion photographs from glossy magazines, or theatre posters is busy enough to take attention away from the uneven surface. Coat the collage with clear sealer to protect it from steam.

Flooring ideas

If the floor is worse for wear, it is fairly cheap and simple to replace it with looselay vinyl sheet.

Alternatively, remove the old covering to expose the floor boards. If they are not too damaged or uneven, sand them down and then varnish or paint them, applying enough coats to make them really waterproof. The idea of painting each board a different shade works well for the floor too. Use the same colour but graduate it from light to dark and back again.

An uneven wooden or chipped tile floor can be disguised with duck boards. These are slatted wood platforms which allow the dust to fall through so the surface always looks neat. You lift up the platforms to sweep underneath. (It can also be used to make a slatted bathmat.)

Important details

The overall look of the bathroom can be improved enormously by paying attention to the details. Buy soaps, tissues and toilet rolls all in the same colour. Toothbrushes, facecloths and towels will get mixed up if they match; but if they are related and co-ordinate with the main colour scheme, they'll be identifiable as well as integrated.

If you buy economy sizes of shampoo and bath salts, decant them into classy-looking glass or ceramic containers. Put talc from family-size tins into a glass bowl and add a down or lambswool puff for a touch of unashamed luxury.

Left: Ornaments and accessories are as important in the bathroom as in any other room and can do a lot to dress up old fittings.

Index

DATE			
2-8-89			
FEB. 18 1992			
OCT. 15 1992			